THE HILLSBOROUGH ENCYCLOPEDIA

ACKNOWLEDGEMENTS

The author wishes to thank Sheffield Wednesday FC and the Association of Statisticians for their help in producing this book and all at Mainstream Publishing for their support in producing books in this series.

PHOTOGRAPHS

The photographs in this book have been supplied by the *Lancashire Evening Post*, the *Liverpool Daily Post* and *Echo*, the Smith Davis Press Agency and from the author's personal collection. All cigarette cards are reproduced from the collection of Peter Stafford.

THE
HILLSBOROUGH
ENCYCLOPEDIA

An A-Z of Sheffield Wednesday FC

Dean Hayes

MAINSTREAM
PUBLISHING

EDINBURGH AND LONDON

First published in Great Britain in 1999 by
MAINSTREAM PUBLISHING COMPANY (EDINBURGH) LTD
7 Albany Street
Edinburgh EH1 3UG

This edition 2002

ISBN 1 85158 960 0

A catalogue record for this book is available from the British Library

Printed in Great Britain by Antony Rowe Ltd, Eastbourne

ABANDONED MATCHES. When Wednesday entertained Aston Villa at Olive Grove on 26 November 1898, the referee, Arthur Scragg, arrived late and so the game had to be abandoned after 79 minutes because of bad light, with the score at 3–1 in Wednesday's favour. Instead of allowing the result to stand, the League Management Committee ordered the remaining 11 minutes to be played at a later date. So play resumed on 13 March 1899 and Wednesday, in the shape of Richards, scored an extra goal to make it 4–1 for the Sheffield side. It was the shortest ever match in football league history and was followed by the two sides playing a benefit match in front of the 3,000 crowd.

AGGREGATE SCORE. Sheffield Wednesday's highest aggregate score in any competition came in the League Cup competition of 1986–87. Playing Stockport County, the Owls notched up ten goals over the two legs. They won the first leg at Hillsborough 3–0 and then 7–0 at Edgeley Park, where Colin Walker grabbed a hat-trick after coming on as substitute.

ALLEN, JACK. Jack Allen arrived at Wednesday from Brentford as an inside-forward in March 1927, and was in and out of the side until he was converted to centre-forward, although he scored some vital goals towards the end of the 1927–28 season. His first game at centre-forward was at Portsmouth in October 1928 when he scored one of the goals in Wednesday's 3–2 defeat. A week later, he scored three against Birmingham City and followed that with all four goals against Bury at Gigg Lane. Before the turn of the year, he had scored 22 goals in 14 appearances in his new position, including 13 goals in seven consecutive games, ending the season as top scorer with 35 league and Cup goals. Not surprisingly, Wednesday won the league championship and did so again the following season, when Allen netted 39 goals, including four against Manchester United and hat-tricks against Leicester City and Derby County. After scoring 85 goals in 114 first-team appearances, he fell out of favour with the club and was allowed to join Newcastle United. In his first season with the Magpies, he helped them win the FA Cup, scoring the goal from the 'over the line' cross that defeated Arsenal. He later played for Bristol Rovers, ending his career with Gateshead.

ANDERSON, VIV. The first coloured footballer to play league football for Nottingham Forest, he made his league debut against Sheffield Wednesday in September 1974. Nicknamed 'Spider' because of his long legs, he made his England debut against Czechoslovakia in 1978 and so became the first coloured player to gain a full England cap. He remained Forest's regular right-back until the summer of 1984 when, after playing in 430 league and Cup games, he joined Arsenal for £250,000. In his time at the City Ground, he had won a league championship medal, two League Cup winners' medals and was a member of two European Cup winning sides. After appearing in 150 games for the Gunners, he joined Manchester United, again for £250,000, the fee being fixed by an independent tribunal. Plagued by injuries, he joined Sheffield Wednesday in January 1991. He helped the Owls win the second division championship in 1991–92 and spent a further

Viv Anderson

two seasons at Hillsborough, playing in 69 league games and scoring eight goals, before becoming Bryan Robson's assistant-manager at Middlesbrough.

ANGLO-ITALIAN TOURNAMENT. The Owls participated in the experimental Anglo-Italian tournament at the end of the 1969–70 season. Their results were as follows:

Napoli   home   (won 4–3)   away   (lost 1–5)
Juventus home   (drew 0–0)   away   (lost 0–2)

Napoli reached the final but were losing 3–0 to Swindon Town when after 79 minutes the game was abandoned owing to crowd trouble.

APPEARANCES. Andrew Wilson holds the record for the most appearances in a Sheffield Wednesday shirt, with a total of 546 games to his credit between 1900 and 1920. In all, Wilson played 502 league games and 44 FA Cup games.

ASHURST, LEN. Liverpool-born Len Ashurst made his name as a constructive full-back for Sunderland, making 410 league appearances for the Roker Park club, before moving to Hartlepool United as player-manager in March 1971. In the summer of 1974, he became manager of Gillingham, joining Sheffield Wednesday in October 1975. Though he was unable to get the Owls out of the third division, he did make a number of important signings which were of long-term benefit to the Hillsborough club, including Jeff Johnson and Bob Bolder. When he left two years later, the club were firmly rooted to the foot of the third division without a win in their first ten games. He later managed Newport County, leading the Ironsides to promotion, the Welsh Cup and entry into Europe before moving to Cardiff City and helping the Ninian Park club to promotion

Len Ashurst

7

from the third division. He had an unhappy spell at his former club Sunderland before going abroad to coach in Kuwait and Qatar. He returned to these shores to become assistant-manager at Blackpool before taking full charge at Cardiff City.

ATHERTON, PETER. He made his league debut for Wigan Athletic at Blackpool in October 1987, prior to signing professional forms for the Latics. After claiming a regular place the following season, Atherton did not miss another match for the Springfield Park club, apart from one when he was substitute, until he signed for Coventry City for £300,000 in August 1991. He had played in 178 first team games. Within two months of arriving at Highfield Road, he had been selected for the England Under-21 side. A tenacious defender, he played

Peter Atherton

in 120 games for the Sky Blues before joining Sheffield Wednesday in June 1994 for £800,000. He made his debut for the Owls against Tottenham Hotspur in the opening game of the 1994–95 season and missed only one game, the 7–1 home defeat by Nottingham Forest. Midway through the following season, he was appointed captain by David Pleat. The Orrell-born defender could inspire his colleagues by his never-say-die attitude.

ATKINSON, RON. After failing to make the grade at Aston Villa, Atkinson was given a free transfer and joined Headington United, soon to change their name to Oxford United in 1959. They won two Southern league championships, on both occasions captained by Atkinson. Admitted to the Football League in 1962, Atkinson led them to promotion from the fourth division in 1965 and into the second divsion three years later. He served Oxford for 15 years, playing in 560 matches, 383 of them in the League. After a short spell in charge of Kettering, he took over as manager of Cambridge United and led them to the fourth division championship before joining West Bromwich Albion. After the Baggies had finished third in the first division, he moved to Manchester United. The Red Devils won the FA Cup in 1983 and 1985, but in 1986 Big Ron was sacked, receiving £100,000 in compensation. He joined Spanish club Atletico Madrid but after 96 days he was dismissed despite taking the club to third position. He returned to England as caretaker-manager of Sheffield Wednesday in February 1989. He saved the club from relegation and was persuaded to take the post permanently in the

Ron Atkinson

summer. At the end of the following season, the Owls were rather unluckily relegated, though in 1990–91 they returned to the first division and won the League Cup, beating Manchester United in the final. Before he could enjoy the victory, Atkinson moved to Aston Villa. In 1992–93, they were runners-up in the Premier League and winners of the League Cup the following season. He left Villa Park in November 1994, later becoming manager of Coventry City.

ATTENDANCE – AVERAGE. The average home league attendances for Sheffield Wednesday over the last ten seasons have been as follows:

1987–88	19,796	1992–93	27,263
1988–89	20,037	1993–94	27,187
1989–90	20,930	1994–95	25,323
1990–91	26,605	1995–96	24,877
1991–92	29,560	1996–97	25,693

ATTENDANCE – HIGHEST. The record attendance at Hillsborough is 72,841 for the fifth round FA Cup game with Manchester City on 17 February 1934. The match ended in a 2–2 draw but Wednesday lost the replay at Maine Road 2–0. The record attendance for a league match is 65,384 who, on 5

January 1952, watched Sheffield Wednesday lose 3–1 to rivals Sheffield United with Derek Dooley scoring for the Owls.

ATTENDANCE – LOWEST. The lowest attendance at Hillsborough, although the ground was known as Owlerton until 1914, was 2,500 for the visit of Everton on 5 April 1902, a game which ended all square at 1–1.

AWAY MATCHES. Sheffield Wednesday's best away wins have come in the League Cup when they won 8–0 at Aldershot in 1989–90 and 7–0 at Stockport County in 1986–87. The Owls also won 7–2 at Manchester United in a fourth round FA Cup replay. The club's best away win in the League is 6–0, a scoreline achieved at Nottingham Forest in 1909–10 and at West Ham United in 1951–52. Wednesday's worst defeat away from home is 10–0 by Aston Villa in 1912–13. The highest scoring away match that Wednesday have been involved in was in 1931–32 when they went down 9–3 to Everton at Goodison Park.

AWAY SEASONS. The club's highest number of away wins came in 1929–30 when they won 11 of their 21 matches when winning the first division championship. The club failed to win an away game in five seasons: 1898–99, 1900–01, 1926–27, 1957–58 and 1975–76.

B

BALL, JACK. Southport-born Jack Ball arrived from Manchester United in July 1930 and made his Wednesday debut in a 1–1 draw at home to Chelsea in September of that year. He proved to be a prolific goalscorer and in his first 14 matches, scored 17 goals, including hat-tricks against Sunderland (home 7–2) and Leicester City (away 5–2), ending the season as the club's top scorer with 27 goals in 36 league appearances. In 1931–32, Ball scored 23 league goals, 11 of which were from the penalty spot – an achievement which remained a league record for over 40 years. His best season for the club was 1932–33 when he scored 35 goals in 42 league and Cup appearances, with 33 of them coming in the League. He scored four goals in Wednesday's 5–3 win at Wolverhampton Wanderers and another hat-trick against Leicester City. When Billy Walker took over as Wednesday's manager in 1933, he decided that at the end of the year, Ball could return to Old Trafford in exchange for Neil Dewar. Ball had scored 94 goals in 135 appearances with many of his strikes coming in the closing minutes of a game. After nine months at Old Trafford, he had a short spell with Huddersfield Town before playing for Luton Town. When his playing days were over, he went to coach in France.

BANNISTER, GARY. Signed from Coventry City for £100,000 in August 1981, Gary Bannister made an immediate impact, scoring

11

22 goals in his first season to become the supporters' Player of the Year. He followed this up with another 22 goals in 1982–83 and 22 again in 1983–84 when Wednesday gained promotion to the first division. One of the club's best-ever buys, the Hillsborough faithful were disappointed when, with a first-division place achieved, he chose to join Queens Park Rangers for £200,000 in the close season. At Loftus Road, he scored 56 goals in 136 league games and helped them reach the League Cup final. He returned to Coventry in March 1988, but two years later left to play for West Bromwich Albion. After a loan spell at Oxford United, he joined Nottingham Forest on a free transfer. The City Ground side finished bottom of the Premier League in 1992–93. He then had spells with Stoke City and Lincoln City before becoming player-coach at Darlington.

BANNISTER, KEITH. After playing in a couple of games during the 1944–45 season, Keith Bannister made his league debut at Bury on Christmas Day 1946, when the Owls went down 4–2. He kept his place for the return fixture on Boxing Day but the Shakers did the double over Wednesday, winning 5–2. Bannister spent two seasons in Wednesday's reserve side and was in and out of the first team for three years before replacing Jackson in October 1951. He went on to play in 31 consecutive league games and, having been made captain, lifted the second division championship shield at the end of the season. Yet despite his outstanding performances during that championship winning campaign, he played in only one game the following season and in 1953 he joined Chesterfield.

BART-WILLIAMS, CHRIS. A teenage footballing prodigy, at 16 years 232 days, Chris Bart-Williams was the youngest player to make his full debut for Orient, when he played and scored against Tranmere Rovers in February 1991. An automatic choice for the O's the following season, he was signed up by Wednesday manager Trevor Francis in November 1991. A week later, he was making his debut for the Owls against the league champions Arsenal. Although most of his games for Wednesday were in midfield, when he did play up-front, he scored a hat-trick in a 5–2 home win over Southampton. Having earlier played for the England Under-21 side, he played a vital role for his country in the World Youth Cup in Australia, but after appearing in 152 league and Cup games for Wednesday, he joined Nottingham Forest in July 1995 for £2.5 million. Not an immediate first-team choice at the City Ground, he later displaced David Phillips and though he failed to score in his 48 League and Cup games, this was because he was employed as a midfield anchor.

BEESON, GEORGE. Signed from Chesterfield in March 1929, full-back George Beeson spent his first three seasons at Hillsborough as understudy to Tommy Walker. Eventually establishing himself in the Wednesday side in 1932, he impressed so much that he represented the Football League against the Irish League on two occasions. He made just 75 appearances for the Owls in four and a half seasons at the club before joining Aston Villa as part of the deal which brought Joe Nibloe to Hillsborough.

BEST STARTS. Wednesday were unbeaten for the first 15 games of the 1983–84 second division promotion winning season, when they won 11 and drew four of their matches. Their first defeat came at Crystal Palace on 26 November when they went down 1–0.

BETTS, BILLY. Known as 'Old Warhorse', Billy Betts played his first game for Wednesday in January 1883 but after just three FA Cup games, left the club to assist Lockwood Brothers. He was one of their best players, instrumental in them winning both the Sheffield Challenge Cup and Wharncliffe Charity Cup in 1884. In 1887, he starred in the FA Cup quarter-final matches against West Bromwich Albion before returning to Wednesday at the outset of the Olive Grove era. In February 1889, he played for England in their 4–1 defeat of Wales at Stoke's Victoria Ground and had the distinction of appearing in Wednesday's first FA Cup final against Blackburn Rovers in 1890 and the club's first football league match. He continued to play for Wednesday until 1895, when he lost his place to Tommy Crawshaw who had joined the club from Heywood Central the year before.

BINKS, SID. Entering the game late, Sid Binks played for Bishop Auckland at the end of the First World War and won an FA

Amateur Cup winners' medal with the Durham side as well as gaining an England amateur international cap. He joined Wednesday in the summer of 1922, being persuaded by Owls' manager Bob Brown to turn professional. A big, bustling centre-forward, he made his debut in the opening game of the 1922–23 season, scoring the winning goal at Rotherham. He ended the season with 13 goals, joint top scorer along with Smailes and Taylor. The following season he headed the Wednesday scoring charts with 16 goals, including four in a 6–0 win over Crystal Palace and three in a 3–2 win at Bristol City. Popular with the Wednesday fans, it came as a great surprise in November 1924 when he was exchanged for Huddersfield's Ted Richardson. He later played for Blackpool, Portsmouth, Southend and Fulham, ending his career as a centre-half with Chesterfield.

BIRCH, ARNOLD. Goalkeeper Arnold Birch made 23 appearances for Wednesday in wartime games before making his League debut in the opening game of the 1919–20 season. He played in 21 league games during that campaign but in the three seasons that followed, his appearances were restricted to just six. In the main, that was due to the splendid form of Teddy Davison and so in June 1923, Birch moved to Chesterfield. At Saltergate in 1923–24, he set a league record for a goalkeeper by scoring from the penalty spot on five occasions.

BLAIR, ANDY. Joining Coventry City straight from school, the Kirkcaldy-born midfielder won five Under-21 caps for Scotland before signing for Aston Villa in the summer of 1981. However, competition for places in Villa's midfield was tough and after appearing in only 33 league games he joined Wednesday for £50,000, one-seventh of the fee he had cost Villa when they bought him from Coventry. He missed only one game in 1984–85, Wednesday's first season back in the top flight since 1969–70. In that season's League Cup tie with Luton Town on 20 November 1984, he wrote himself into the record books when he scored a hat-trick of penalties in Wednesday's 4–2 win. Midway through the following season, his form deteriorated and he rejoined Aston Villa. Hampered by injuries, he went on loan to Barnsley before ending his career with Northampton Town.

BLAIR, JIMMY. Full-back Jimmy Blair was one of the best in the game when Wednesday paid Clyde £2,000 for his services in July 1914. However, though he stayed with the club until November 1920, he played in only 61 first-team games. The circumstances that prevented him playing in more games were, to say the least, unfortunate. Within weeks of his arrival at Hillsborough, he was involved in a motor-cycle accident and forced to miss the opening games of the 1914–15 season. He eventually made his debut in a 6–0 win over Bradford at the end of September, but was soon injured again and appeared in only 20 games before war broke out. Having gone back to Scotland, he took some persuading to return to Hillsborough when football resumed in 1919–20. When he did so, he found himself playing in a Wednesday side that was relegated to the second division. Yet despite this, he won two caps for Scotland, the second in the epic 5–4 England win at Hillsborough. He joined Cardiff City the following season and was an important member of the Welsh club's side that reached the FA Cup Final of 1925.

BLENKINSOP, ERNEST. One of the best full-backs the club has ever had, Ernest Blenkinsop was working at Brierley Colliery when Hull City signed him for £100 and 80 pints of beer. He joined Wednesday in January 1923 for a fee of £1,000 and over the next 12 seasons went on to appear in 424 league and Cup games for the Owls. He won the first of 26 England caps in 1928 when he played in the 3–1 win over Belgium in Antwerp. Along with Strange, Marsden and Rimmer, he played in England's 5–2 victory over Scotland at Wembley in 1930. He later captained England twice against the Scots before losing his place to Arsenal's Eddie Hapgood. Blenkinsop had superb ball control and was an immaculate distributor of the ball. He won a second division championship medal in 1925–26 and league championship medals in 1928–29 and 1929–30. Soon after Billy Walker was appointed Wednesday manager, 'Blenkie' was allowed to leave Hillsborough and joined Liverpool for £6,500. It was a decision that angered a good number of the Wednesday supporters who let the new Wednesday boss know that they felt he had made a big mistake.

BLINKER, REGI. A Dutch international winger, Blinker was signed from Feyenoord for £275,000 in March 1996. He made a goalscoring debut for the Owls at Villa Park, scoring both Wednesday's goals in a 3–2 defeat. The Hillsborough fans took to him immediately because the Dutchman brought flair to a Wednesday side whose play was becoming very predictable. In 1996–97, he appeared in almost every game, though on many occasions as a substitute. He didn't score his first goal of the season until the Owls' 3–0 win at Nottingham Forest in March 1997. In August 1997 he transferred to Celtic.

BOLDER, BOB. Signed from Dover FC in March 1977, goalkeeper Bob Bolder was given his chance under the managership of Jack Charlton and made his debut in a 1–0 win over Rotherham United. The Wednesday manager was convinced that Chris Turner's lack of inches gave him a disadvantage and so continued to play Bolder despite adverse criticism. However, after Bolder had a nightmare game in the 3–0 defeat at Hillsborough against Blackburn Rovers on 25 August 1979, he had no option but to drop him. Bolder bounced back and in 1981–82 and 1982–83 was an ever-present playing in 116 consecutive league games before joining Liverpool in the summer of 1983. He never played in the senior side at Anfield and two years later signed for Sunderland. After one season at Roker Park in which he appeared in 22 league games, he transferred to Charlton Athletic. The first choice keeper for the Addicks, he played in 249 League games before hanging up his boots.

BOOKS. Among the books that have been written about Sheffield Wednesday Football Club are:
The Romance of The Wednesday 1867–1926 by Richard A. Sparling (Leng, 1926).
Football in Sheffield by Percy M.Young (Stanley Paul, 1962).
Let's Talk about Sheffield Wednesday by Tom Morgan (Sentinel, 1946).
Sheffield Wednesday. A Complete Record 1867–1987 by Keith Farnsworth (Breedon, 1987).

BOOTH, ANDY. Starting his league career with his home-town club Huddersfield Town, Andy Booth shot to fame in the 1994–95 season, scoring 27 league and Cup goals, including hat-tricks against Plymouth Argyle and Chester City. It was this sort of form that had a host of Premier League clubs chasing after his signature. Good in the air, he had played in 151 games for the Terriers and scored 64 goals when Wednesday secured his services for £2.7 million in the summer of 1996. An England Under-21 international, he made his Wednesday debut in the opening game of the 1996–97 season against Aston Villa, scoring his first goal for the club in the next game at Leeds United.

BRADSHAW, FRANK. Despite scoring two goals on his Wednesday debut in a 3–1 win over Everton in April 1906, Bradshaw had to wait a further two seasons before winning a regular place in the first team. He was a prolific goalscorer in the club's reserve side and helped them win the Midland League in 1905–06. Bradshaw was a member of the Wednesday side that won the FA Cup in 1907, beating Everton 2–1 in the final, yet it was only his fourth first-team appearance. In December 1907, he scored a hat-trick in Wednesday's 6–0 win over Woolwich Arsenal and ended the season with 12 goals in 30 appearances. At the end of the campaign, he was selected for England against Austria in Vienna and marked his debut with a hat-trick in a 1–1 win. Selected to play against Ireland the following February, he was forced to cry off because of injury and never got another chance at international level. It was at around this time that he suffered from knee trouble and was allowed to join Northampton Town, then members of the Southern League. In 1911, he moved back into league circles with Everton before playing for Arsenal. He made over 200 appearances for the first division sides before leaving the game in 1923. Many of his games with the London club were played at full-back, though he had scored over 70 league goals from the centre-forward position.

BRADY, ALEC. After playing his early football with Burnley and Sunderland, Alec Brady helped Everton win the league championship in 1890–91 before returning to his native Scotland to play for Celtic. He helped the Parkhead club win the Scottish Cup in 1892 before being persuaded, along with centre-forward Jack Madden, to come to Sheffield and sign for Wednesday, after they had appeared in a practice match. It transpired that a Roman

Catholic priest had followed the two men from Glasgow to take them back to Celtic. Wednesday agreed that the two men should go into hiding. Madden was found and returned to Scotland, but Brady wasn't and stayed with Wednesday. On 14 October 1893, he became the first Wednesday player to score a hat-trick in the League when Derby County were beaten 4–0. A superb passer of the ball, he won an FA Cup runners-up medal when Wednesday lost to Wolves 2–1 at Crystal Palace. He played the last of his 177 league and Cup games for Wednesday at home to Stoke in January 1899.

BRANDON, HARRY. Harry Brandon made his Wednesday debut in the very first match with Sheffield United, at Olive Grove on 15 December 1890. He had played his early football with Scottish clubs St Mirren and Clyde before moving south and becoming a great favourite with Wednesday's supporters. Although he preferred half-back, he played in a variety of positions and was the club's only representative in the Football Alliance side that played the Football League XI at Olive Grove in 1891. A member of the Wednesday side that won the FA Cup in 1896, he scored 17 goals in 172 league and Cup appearances.

BRANDON, TOM. Beginning his league career with Blackburn Rovers, where he represented the Football League against the Football Alliance, Tom Brandon joined Wednesday in 1892. The cousin of Harry Brandon, he was encouraged to move across the Pennines by a most favourable contract and the promise of a public house in the town. He was Wednesday's captain when the club were admitted to the Football League in 1892 and is credited with the club's first goal in the competition when they beat Notts County 1–0 in their opening match. He scored only two goals for the club, his second coming in the final match of the season, also against Notts County, helping Wednesday to win 3–2 and avoid involvement in the 'Test' matches. At the end of that season, Brandon returned to Blackburn, leaving Wednesday upset at the circumstances of his move.

BRASH, ARCHIE. Archie Brash joined Wednesday from St Mirren in 1894, making his debut in the opening game of the 1894–95 season at Everton. Though on the small side, his speed and skill often made him a matchwinner. During Wednesday's FA Cup run of 1895–96, Brash turned in a number of memorable performances, perhaps none more so than in the quarter-final tie against Everton, where he created two goals for Laurie Bell and scored two himself in a 4–1 win. In the semi-final at Goodison Park, it was his goal that gave Wednesday a draw in the game with Bolton, and he created the goals that gave the Owls a 3–1 win in the replay. Following relegation in 1898–99 he helped the club to win the second division championship at the first time of asking but in the summer of 1900, he left Wednesday to join Leicester Fosse.

BRAYSHAW, TEDDY. The son of a well-known Sheffield detective, Teddy Brayshaw joined Wednesday in 1884 and was a member of the pressure group that tried to make the club adopt professionalism. In 1887, he was capped by England against Ireland at Bramall Lane and starred in a 7–0 win. In fact, he was so proud of his international cap that he insisted on wearing it when playing for Wednesday for months afterwards. A member of the side that played in the first match at Olive Grove, he was also instrumental in the club reaching its first FA Cup final, in 1890. The following year, he suffered a bad foot injury and had to retire.

BRIGHT, MARK. An unselfish striker, Mark Bright made his debut for Port Vale in May 1982 and although he could not command a regular place at Vale Park, he did enough to impress Gordon Milne who signed him for Leicester City. During his stay at Filbert Street, Bright was very much in the shadows of Gary Lineker and Alan Smith and after two seasons, moved to Crystal Palace for just £75,000. It proved to be a bargain signing, as the Stoke-born player formed a lethal striking partnership with Ian Wright. Even when Wright joined Arsenal in September 1991, Bright continued to score goals and in 1991–92, he top scored with 20 league and Cup goals after appearing in each one of the club's 54 games. However, after just four games of the following season, he was transferred to Sheffield Wednesday in exchange for Paul Williams and £1,375,000. He immediately settled in at Hillsborough and was the Owls' leading scorer in 1992–93. Now playing for Charlton Athletic, his goals per game ratio of 66 goals in 166 games over five seasons, bears comparison with most Premiership strikers.

Mark Bright

BRITTLETON, TOM. The oldest player ever to appear in a Sheffield Wednesday team, Tom Brittleton was 41 years old when he played his last game for the club against Oldham Athletic in May 1920. He had joined the club from Stockport County in January 1905 as an inside-forward, though he subsequently went on to appear in a variety of positions for the Owls over the next 15 years. There is no doubt that he gave his best performances as a wing-half, where he developed into one of the club's earliest exponents of the long throw-in. He captained Wednesday on a number of occasions and in 1912 won the first of five England caps when he played against Ireland. He could have won more representative honours, but Brittleton was his own man. On one occasion, he turned down the chance of touring South Africa with an FA XI, preferring to stay at home and spend his time fishing. Even after playing his last game for Wednesday, he joined Stoke and helped the Potters win promotion to the first division in 1921–22.

BROTHERS. There have been a number of sets of brothers who have played for Wednesday. Tom Brandon who captained Wednesday at the time of their admission to the Football League and who is credited with the club's first goal in the competition, played in 37 league and Cup games before returning to Blackburn Rovers. His brothers Jim and Bob also played for Wednesday. Tom McAnearney played in 382 games for the Owls, helping them to win the second division championship in 1955–56 and 1958–59. His brother Jim never got the same chance to establish himself and was restricted to 40 outings at first-team level over six seasons. The two brothers lined up together in the same Wednesday side on 26 occasions. Derek Wilkinson gave Wednesday great service, playing in 233 games and scoring 57 goals. An important member of the club's 1958–59 second division championship-winning side, his twin brother Eric appeared just once in the first team, playing alongside him at Sunderland in September 1958. Goalkeeping brothers Ron and Peter Springett occupied the number one shirt between them from March 1957 to December 1974. England international Ron Springett made 384 appearances between 1957 and 1967 and brother Peter, 207 appearances from 1967 to 1974. Both began their careers at Queens Park Rangers, Peter coming to

Hillsborough when Ron returned to Loftus Road in a unique deal in June 1967.

BROWN, ALAN. After beginning his playing career with Huddersfield Town, Alan Brown made a name for himself when he joined Burnley and was captain and centre-half when they won promotion and reached the FA Cup final in 1947. After a short spell with Notts County, he joined Wednesday as first-team coach, a position he held from January 1951 to August 1954. He returned to Burnley for his first managerial post but in 1957 came back to Hillsborough for another spell as Wednesday's coach before moving on to manage Sunderland a few months later. After Sunderland were relegated for the first time in their history at the end of the 1957–58 season, Brown finally led them back to the top flight in 1964 after going close on a number of occasions. Rather than enjoy his success, Brown moved back to Hillsborough to manage Wednesday. In 1966, the club reached the FA Cup final only to lose 3–2 to Everton after being two goals up. In February 1968, with the Owls perilously close to the foot of the first division, Brown left the club after receiving an offer to return to Sunderland.

BROWN, BOB. Brown was the first and regarded by many as the most successful, professional secretary–manager in Sheffield Wednesday's history. After leaving school, Brown served an apprenticeship in a shipyard and played soccer for a number of sides in the north east, including Hebburn Argyle. Just after the turn of the century, he joined Wednesday as a scout, later working in the club's offices at Owlerton. In 1911, he was appointed secretary–manager of Southern League Portsmouth and in his first season led them to the second division championship. In 1919–20 he took Pompey to the first division championship before leaving in April 1920 to join Gillingham. He was there for only a few months before joining Wednesday in the close season. However, success took some time to come. The Owls struggled in Brown's first season and between mid-October 1920 and mid-January 1921, won only one out of 15 matches. In 1925–26, Brown turned things round, leading Wednesday to the second division championship. In 1927–28, the club looked set to be relegated but they took 17 points from their last ten games to avoid the drop. The following two campaigns brought nothing but success as they won the league championship in both 1928–29 and 1929–30. In the latter season, Wednesday almost did the double, a controversial Alex Jackson equalising goal in the FA Cup semi-final spurring Huddersfield on to a 2–1 win. There is no doubt that Brown's appointment of Jimmy Seed as captain was a major turning point in the club's fortunes. After five seasons during which the side had not finished below third place in the first division, Brown seemed to lose interest in the job. His wife had died in 1932 and a year later, he resigned due to ill health. When he recovered, he joined Chelsea as a scout, but in March 1935, while on a scouting mission, he collapsed while boarding a train and died in hospital the following day.

BROWN, JACK. Goalkeeper Jack Brown played his early football with Worksop Town and was in the team that held first division giants Tottenham Hotspur to a goalless draw in a first round FA Cup tie at White Hart Lane. Despite conceding nine goals in the replay, Brown received national acclaim and was more than happy when Wednesday paid £300 for his services in February 1923. A brave and fearless goalkeeper, he had to wait until 1925–26 before it could be said that he was Wednesday's first choice, as veteran Teddy Davison kept his place. In 1925–26, Brown was an ever-present and kept 16 clean sheets as Wednesday won the second division championship. In 1927, he won the first of six England caps when he played in the 3–3 draw with Wales at Wrexham. He was an ever-present again in 1928–29 when the Owls won the league championship and missed just one game the following season when they retained the title. In 1935 he kept goal as Wednesday beat West Bromwich Albion 4–2 to win the FA Cup. He was Wednesday's first choice keeper for 12 seasons, playing in 507 league and Cup games before losing his place towards the end of the 1936–37 season.

BUCKINGHAM, VIC. He made his debut for Tottenham Hotspur against Bury in 1935, and soon became established at half-back but, like so many others of his generation, the best years of Buckingham's career were lost to the war. Serving in the RAF, he guested for other clubs and appeared for England in two wartime internationals against Wales. In 1947–48 he was a division two

23

ever-present but early in the 1949–50 season, he retired after 16 years at White Hart Lane. He never played in the first division, a record which may show why this tall, stylish player later sought and achieved success as a coach and manager. He took to coaching Spurs' juniors but in June 1951, his talents were recognised by Bradford Park Avenue and he became their manager. In February he took over at West Bromwich Albion and in his first year they won the FA Cup and finished runners-up in division one. On leaving the Hawthorns, he coached Ajax of Amsterdam before returning to England to manage Sheffield Wednesday. In each of his three seasons at Hillsborough, the Owls finished in the top half of the first division and also reached the quarter-finals of the Inter Cities Fairs Cup. Yet he was not considered a success and in March 1964, he was dismissed. He was the Wednesday manager during the bribery scandal which resulted in Tony Kay, 'Bronco' Layne and Peter Swan being banned for life. In January 1965 he joined Fulham but after three years of struggling to avoid relegation, he left. He later managed Ethnikos of Greece and Spanish clubs Barcelona and Seville.

BURGESS, HARRY. A prolific goalscorer with Stockport County, where he lined up with former Bolton marksman Joe Smith, Harry Burgess joined Wednesday in 1929. He scored on his debut in a 3–1 win at Aston Villa and ended the season with 19 goals in 39 games as Wednesday won the league championship. In 1930–31, he netted a hat-trick in a 4–0 win at Blackpool and won the first of his four caps against Northern Ireland. In 1933–34, he top scored for Wednesday with 12 goals in the League, yet surprisingly in March 1935 after scoring 77 goals in 234 appearances, he was sold to Chelsea.

BURROWS, HORACE. Following spells with Coventry City and Mansfield Town, wing-half Horace Burrows joined Wednesday in May 1931. It was 1933 before he won a regular place in the Wednesday side but once he did, he played in 121 consecutive league games, being an ever-present in seasons 1933–34 and 1934–35. During this spell, he won three full caps for England and played an important role in helping Wednesday win the FA Cup in 1935. A most creative and talented player, he missed a number of games through injury over the next two seasons but, once fully fit, was an ever-present in 1938–39 when the Owls finished third in division two. He played in 45 wartime games for Wednesday before hanging up his boots.

BURTENSHAW, STEVE. As a player, Steve Burtenshaw served Brighton and Hove Albion as a wing-half for 14 seasons, making 237 league appearances and winning a third division championship medal in 1957–58. When he retired, he took on the job of reserve-team coach at Arsenal, and later chief coach when Don Howe left Highbury. After a short spell coaching Queens Park Rangers, he moved into management with Sheffield Wednesday. His first game in charge at Hillsborough was the first league game to be played on a Sunday at the ground. Wednesday beat Bristol City 3–1. After that, victories were hard to come by, with the Owls winning only 14 of his 70-odd games in charge. They just missed relegation in April 1974 by winning their last game 1–0 at home to Bolton Wanderers, but went down the following season. The club won only five games all season and collected just 21 points to finish bottom of the second division. After a poor start to the 1975–76 season, Burtenshaw's contract was terminated. He had a spell as manager of Queens Park Rangers but that, too, ended in disaster as the Loftus Road club were relegated at the end of his first season.

BURTON, HARRY. When Ambrose Langley hung up his boots following a bad knee injury at Sunderland, Harry Burton proved to be his natural replacement. He had made his first-team debut a week earlier. Forming a solid full-back pairing with Willie Layton, he was a member of the Wednesday side that won the FA Cup in 1907. Burton played in 198 league and Cup games for the Owls with one of his last games for the club being the 1–0 third round FA Cup defeat at home to Glossop North End. Burton conceded the penalty that gave the visitors their goal and to compound matters, missed a spot-kick at the other end of the ground. The following month he joined West Bromwich Albion along with winger George Simpson.

C

CAMPBELL, JIMMY. Born in Leith, Jimmy Campbell arrived at Owlerton in 1911 with a reputation as one of the finest young half-backs in Scotland. He made his debut for Wednesday in the 1–0 win over Bury on 18 February 1911 and played in 110 consecutive league games immediately after making his debut. During that time he turned in some impressive performances and won an international cap when chosen for the match against Wales in 1913. At the outbreak of the First World War, he was called up for military service and after spending four years overseas, he returned to Hillsborough a shadow of his former self. In the Owls' disastrous 1919–20 season, when they finished bottom of the first division, he made 25 appearances and scored in Wednesday's 2–1 win over Sheffield United. Former Wednesday player, Ambrose Langley who was manager of Huddersfield Town, took him to Leeds Road, but the popular Scot's health was already deteriorating and he was forced to retire. He died in May 1925, aged 38.

CAPACITY. The total capacity of Hillsborough in 1996–97 was 39,859 all-seated.

CAPS. The most capped player in the club's history is Nigel Worthington who won 50 caps for Northern Ireland.

CAPS – ENGLAND. The first Sheffield Wednesday player to be capped by England was Charles Clegg when he played against Scotland in 1872. The most capped player is Ron Springett with 33 caps.

CAPS – NORTHERN IRELAND. The first Sheffield Wednesday player to be capped by Northern Ireland was English McConnell when he played against Scotland in 1909. The most capped player is Nigel Worthington with 50 caps.

CAPS – SCOTLAND. The first Sheffield Wednesday player to be capped by Scotland was Jack Lyall when he played against England in 1905. The most capped player is Andrew Wilson with six caps.

CAPS – WALES. The first Sheffield Wednesday player to be capped by Wales was Rees Williams when he played against Scotland in 1923. The most capped player is Peter Rodrigues with 16 caps.

CAPTAINS. Among the many players who have captained the club are Tom Brandon, who was captain at the time of the club's admission to the Football League in 1892. In most records, he is credited with the club's first goal which won them their first league match at Notts County. Jack Earp was captain of the first Wednesday team to win the FA Cup in 1896 when they beat Wolverhampton Wanderers 2–1. Tommy Crawshaw played in two FA Cup winning sides for Wednesday, captaining them to a 2–1 victory over Everton in the 1907 final. He also played in the league championship winning teams in 1902–03 and 1903–04. Always leading by example, no one fought harder when things weren't going their way. Jimmy Seed led the Owls to successive league championships in 1928–29 and 1929–30. He took over as captain from Fred Kean in 1927–28 and inspired the club to their 'Great Escape' that season. Ronnie Starling captained Sheffield Wednesday when they beat West Bromwich Albion 4–2 at Wembley in 1935. After replacing Tom McAnearney as captain, Don Megson led the Owls out at Wembley in the 1966 FA Cup final and took the team on an unprecedented losers' lap of honour.

CATLIN, TED. After making his Wednesday debut against Leicester City in March 1931, for his second appearance Ted Catlin replaced the injured Ernest Blenkinsop at Goodison Park, where Everton beat the Owls 9–3. When Blenkinsop joined Liverpool, Catlin came into his own and was a member of the Wednesday side that won the FA Cup in 1935. In 1936–37, Catlin missed only two league games during a season in which he was capped five times by England and appeared for the Football League. When war broke out, Catlin had played in 227 league and Cup games for Wednesday. He continued to play in another 92 wartime games including the final of the League North War Cup in 1943. Despite being injured in the first leg, he managed one more season for the Owls, playing his last game in a 6–1 home defeat by Mansfield Town.

CATTERICK, HARRY. As a player at Goodison Park, Harry Catterick was understudy to Tommy Lawton and Jock Dodds and in 14 years at the club was limited to 71 appearances. In December 1951, he became player-manager of Crewe Alexandra but two years later moved to Rochdale, where he developed the Spotland club's first successful side for many seasons. Catterick joined Sheffield Wednesday in August 1958 and established his reputation as the Owls gained promotion to division one in his first season in charge. In 1960, he led the club to the semi-finals of the FA Cup and in 1960–61, Wednesday finished runners-up to Spurs in the first division. His sudden departure in April 1961 disappointed the Wednesday fans but he was probably frustrated by the lack of money to buy new players. He was out of work for only ten days before being offered the Everton job. After guiding the Blues to fourth place in the first division in his first season, the revival Catterick had sparked reached its climax as Everton won the title. In 1966, he led the club to victory over Wednesday in one of the most exciting post-war FA Cup finals. By the start of the 1969–70 season, Harry Catterick had built one of the finest sides in post-war English football and it came as no surprise when they swept to the title. In January 1972, while driving home from Sheffield, he had a heart attack. In April 1973 with four years of his contract still to run, he was moved sideways into a senior executive role. He died at Goodison Park after an FA Cup quarter-final match against Ipswich Town in March 1985.

CAWLEY, TOM. One of the greatest players in the club's early history, Tom Cawley helped save the club from extinction in 1877 when, despite being a founder member of Sheffield Rovers, he persuaded his fellow rebels to give Wednesday a last chance to adopt professionalism. A regular of the Sheffield FA's inter-association games, he scored seven goals, including a hat-trick against Upton Park in Wednesday's run to their first ever FA Cup final in 1882. He repeated the feat in 1890, scoring another seven goals in the club's run to their second final. Unfortunately, both finals ended in defeat and both to Blackburn Rovers. At the end of that season, he was awarded a benefit, which raised £182 and he was presented with a gold watch and chain for his services to the club. When his playing days were over, he remained a loyal clubman for a good number of years, helping to coach the club's reserve side.

CENTENARY. Sheffield Wednesday celebrated their 100th birthday on 5 September 1967. The following evening for a match against Fulham, they allowed half-price admission throughout the ground. Wednesday won 4–2 with goals from Ritchie 2, Mobley and Ford in front of a crowd of 26,551 which was much lower than the two previous home games!

CENTRAL LEAGUE. The Central League was formed in 1911 by the Northern and Midland giants of the Football League as a reserve-team league. Sheffield Wednesday have won the central league championship on four occasions, in 1928–29, 1945–46, 1960–61 and 1990–91.

CENTURIES. Eight individual players have scored 100 or more league goals for Sheffield Wednesday. Andrew Wilson is the greatest goalscorer with 199 strikes in his Hillsborough career (1900–1920). Other centurions are John Fantham (147), Redfern Froggatt (140), Mark Hooper (125), Ellis Rimmer (122), Jimmy Trotter (109), David Hirst (104), and Fred Spiksley (100). Mark Hooper holds the club record for the most consecutive league appearances – 174. Other players to have made over 100 consecutive appearances during their careers are Martin Hodge (173), Hugh Swift (132), Horace Burrows (121), Don Megson (119), Bob Bolder (116), Vic Mobley (113), Jimmy Campbell (110), and Ellis Rimmer (110).

CHAMBERLAIN, MARK. After joining Stoke City from Port Vale in August 1982 for £125,000, Mark Chamberlain had played in only 18 senior games for the Victoria Ground club before making his full international debut for England. He went on to win eight caps before joining Sheffield Wednesday for £350,000 in September 1985. The bulk of his appearances for the club were as substitute and in August 1988 after appearing in 66 league games, of which 34 were as substitute, he moved to Portsmouth. After making 167 league appearances for Pompey, he joined Brighton and Hove Albion.

CHAMPIONSHIPS. Sheffield Wednesday have won the league championship on four occasions. The first of these was in 1902–03, when the Owls beat both Aston Villa and Sunderland by just one point. Wednesday had finished their league programme but Sunderland still had to play at Newcastle United, where the Roker Park club surprisingly lost. Wednesday retained the league championship the following season, finishing three points clear of Manchester City, and were undefeated at home. The Owls won the league championship a third time in 1928–29, with Jack Allen scoring 33 goals, including 13 in a run of seven consecutive games. The club last won the title in 1929–30, repeating their achievement of the early part of the century by winning two league championships in successive years.

CHAPMAN, HARRY. The brother of the great manager, Herbert Chapman, Harry was probably the greatest uncapped inside-forward of his day and if Derby County's Steve Bloomer hadn't been on the scene, he would have represented England many times. Joining Wednesday from Worksop in 1900, he was the creator and scorer of goals, winning league championship medals in 1902–03 and 1903–04 and an FA Cup winners' medal in 1907. He played in 298 league and Cup games for the Owls, scoring 102 goals, before, in 1911, moving to play for Hull City.

CHAPMAN, LEE. The son of Roy, who played for Aston Villa and Lincoln, Lee Chapman started his career with Stoke City, although he made his league debut while on loan with

Plymouth Argyle in December 1978. In three seasons at the Victoria Ground, he scored 38 goals in 107 league and Cup appearances before signing for Arsenal. Due to a cartilage operation, he found himself in and out of the Gunners' side and in December 1983 he moved on to Sunderland. He only spent seven months at Roker Park before Len Ashurst sold him to Wednesday for £100,000. Making his debut in the 3–1 home win over Nottingham Forest on the opening day of the 1984–85 season, he

Lee Chapman

proved to be an old-fashioned centre-forward and one of the best headers of a ball. After four good seasons at Hillsborough in which he scored 80 goals in 187 first-team games, he chose to join French club Niort, but they could not pay the modest transfer fee and so he moved to Nottingham Forest. In his first season at the City Ground, his goals helped Forest to third place in the first division and to a League and Simod Cup double. Surprisingly, in January 1990, he was allowed to join Leeds United where, after helping them to promotion from the second division, he spearheaded their successful bid for the 1991–92 league championship. During that championship-winning season, he scored two hat-tricks, one at Hillsborough against Sheffield Wednesday. However, he was placed on the transfer list and in August 1993 he joined Portsmouth, but within a month had moved to West Ham United. Following a loan spell at Southend, he signed for Ipswich Town before returning to Elland Road on loan to play two games in the Premiership and then joining Swansea City on a free transfer.

CHARITY SHIELD. Sheffield Wednesday have appeared twice in the FA Charity Shield – in 1930 as league champions and in 1935 as

31

FA Cup winners. On both occasions, their opponents were Arsenal.

8 October 1930 at Stamford Bridge,   Lost 1–2
23 October 1935 at Highbury,   Won 1–0

CHARLTON, JACK. In a long playing career at Leeds United, Jack Charlton made 629 appearances, scoring 70 goals, mainly from free-kicks and corners. His early career at Elland Road was overshadowed by his brother Bobby at Manchester United, but after John Charles's departure to Juventus, Jack's career came

Jack Charlton

into its own. Under Don Revie, he developed into a fine centre-half, winning 35 caps for England and a World Cup winners' medal in 1966. After Leeds United gained promotion as champions of the second division in 1964, honours came thick and fast, and in 1967 he was voted Footballer of the Year. He retired from playing in May 1973 when he was offered the manager's job at Middlesbrough. By the end of his first season in charge at Ayresome Park, Boro had won the second division championship. After establishing themselves in the top flight, they reached the semi-finals of the League Cup and won the Anglo-Scottish Cup but in April 1977, Charlton resigned. In October 1977, he returned to football as manager of Sheffield Wednesday. They had just gone ten games without a win and looked to be heading for fourth division football, but Charlton led the club to a respectable mid-table position. With such signings as Andy McCulloch and Terry Curran, Charlton created a team which won promotion to division two in 1979–80. Two years later, Wednesday missed further promotion to the first division by one point. However in 1983, just after the Owls had reached the FA Cup semi-finals, Charlton resigned. After a brief spell as caretaker-manager at Middlesbrough, he took control at Newcastle United but it was an unhappy time for the big Geordie and after being barracked by the crowd, he resigned in August 1985. In February 1986 he was approached by the Irish FA to take over the running of the national side on a part-time basis. In 1988, Ireland reached the European Championship finals for the first time and in 1990, the World Cup finals, where they lost 1–0 to Italy in the quarter-finals. Though he led the Irish to the 1994 World Cup finals, they went out to Holland in the second round. In 1995–96, he stepped down to be replaced by Mick McCarthy.

CLEAN SHEET. This is the colloquial expression used to describe a goalkeeper's performance when he does not concede a goal. Three of Sheffield Wednesday's goalkeepers have had 16 clean sheets in a season. They are Jack Lyall in 1903–04, Jack Brown in 1925–26 and Martin Hodge in 1983–84.

CLEGG, CHARLES. Though noted for his work as chairman and later president of the Football Association, Charles Clegg and his brother William played their early football with Wednesday. Charles Clegg played for England in the first match against Scotland in 1872 before becoming a referee. He took charge of a number of international matches and when he turned to administrative work in the mid-1880s, he became something of a national figure. President of the Sheffield and Hallamshire FA for 51 years, Clegg was also chairman and president of Sheffield Wednesday and in 1927 was knighted, partly for his services to the Board of Trade but more for his work in football.

CLEMENTS, DAVE. Northern Ireland international Dave Clements began his career with Wolverhampton Wanderers but, having failed to get a league outing, moved to Coventry City in the summer of 1964. He played in 230 league games for the Sky Blues before signing for Sheffield Wednesday in the £100,000 double deal which also brought Brian Joicey to Hillsborough. A versatile player, he preferred a midfield role and when manager Derek Dooley insisted on playing him at left-back, he became unsettled and asked for a move. Only missing a handful of games in seasons 1971–72 and 1972–73, he had just played in the opening game of the 1973–74 season when Everton signed him for £60,000. On 18 March 1975 while playing for Everton at Middlesbrough, the popular Irishman learned that he had been appointed manager of Northern Ireland. While still in charge of the national side, he joined New York Cosmos. His decision to go to America and play with the legendary Pelé cost him his job as manager of his country.

COCA COLA CUP. See Football League Cup.

COCKCROFT, JOE. After beginning his league career with Rotherham, wing-half Joe Cockcroft had a short spell with Gainsborough Trinity before joining West Ham United. Between 1932 and 1937, Cockcroft played in 217 consecutive league and Cup games for the Hammers to establish a club record. During the early part of the Second World War, his home was blitzed and he returned to live in South Yorkshire and guested for Wednesday. During the war years, he played in 203 games for the Owls and helped them reach the League North War Cup final in 1943, scoring a penalty in the first leg. Cockcroft was a penalty expert, yet after playing in 97 league and Cup games for Wednesday, he transferred to the Blades, whereupon he missed his first penalty for them. In making his debut for Sheffield United he became the oldest player in the history of the game to make his first division debut.

COLOURS. The club colours are blue-and-white striped shirts, blue shorts and blue socks, while their change colours are green shirts, white shorts and white socks. There have been a number of variations over the years with Wednesday playing in white shirts, blue shirts with white sleeves and blue-and-white hooped shirts.

CONSECUTIVE HOME GAMES. Sheffield Wednesday have played an extraordinarily intense sequence of five home games in succession on three occasions, but in 1978–79 they played the five games in the space of just 14 days. They won three, beating Rotherham United 2–1, Swindon Town 2–1 and Blackpool 2–0, but lost to Watford and Hull City both by 3–2.

CONSECUTIVE SCORING – LONGEST SEQUENCE. Derek Dooley holds the club record for consecutive scoring when he was on target in nine consecutive league games, scoring 22 goals in the process. His first came in the 2–2 draw at Queens Park Rangers on 27 October 1951 and the last when he scored all four goals in a 4–0 win over Everton at Hillsborough on 22 December 1951.

CRAIG, BOBBY. Signed from Third Lanark in November 1959, Bobby Craig marked his home debut for Wednesday by scoring one of the goals as the Owls thrashed West Ham United 7–0. The little inside-forward played an important part in the club's successful seasons of 1960–61 and 1961–62 when they were runners-up and sixth in the first division. However, when manager Harry Catterick left to join Everton, Craig found that he did not fit into new manager Vic Buckingham's plans. After losing his place to Colin Dobson, he joined Blackburn Rovers, but had little success there before moving to Oldham Athletic. After scoring four goals in 18 league games for the Latics, he returned to Scotland to play for St Johnstone.

CRAIG, TOMMY. When Tommy Craig joined managerless Sheffield Wednesday in May 1969, he became the club's first £100,000 signing. The former Aberdeen and Scottish Youth captain made his debut in the final game of the 1968–69 season, going on to make 233 appearances over the next six seasons. He was somewhat unlucky to arrive at Hillsborough when Wednesday were struggling, yet Craig's educated left foot both created and scored vital goals. He was made captain of the Scotland Under-23 side and in 1976, when he had joined Newcastle United, he played for the full Scotland side against Switzerland. In December

Tommy Craig

1974 with the Owls sliding towards the third division, manager Steve Burtenshaw regarded him as something of a luxury and sold him to Newcastle United for £120,000. In three years at St James' Park he appeared in 124 league games and scored 22 goals. He later played for Aston Villa, Swansea City and Carlisle United before returning to Scotland to manage Hibernian.

CRAWSHAW, TOMMY. Tommy Crawshaw joined Wednesday from Heywood Central in 1894, immediately succeeding Billy Betts at centre-half. Within 12 months, he had won the first of ten England caps, when he played against Ireland at Derby in March 1895 and made his debut for the Football League. He won two FA Cup winners' medals and two league championship medals in his Wednesday career, captaining the Owls to victory in the second of those FA Cup victories over Everton in 1907. An ever-present in seasons 1899–1900 and 1905–06, he played in 465 league and Cup games for Wednesday over 14 seasons and in his last campaign of 1907–08 was still considered good enough at the age of 35 to play his eighth match for the Football League against the Irish League.

CROMWELL CUP. Oliver Cromwell, manager of the Alexandra Theatre, presented the first Cup which Wednesday ever won. On 15 February 1868 at Bramall Lane, Wednesday under the captaincy of John Marsh beat the Garrick Club 1–0 after extra-time. The trophy is still in the club's possession today.

CUPS. In its history, the club has won eight major trophies: four league championships, three FA Cups and one Football League Cup.

CURRAN, TERRY. A talented, if controversial winger, Terry Curran played league football for 13 clubs. He started his career with Doncaster Rovers, going on to play for Nottingham Forest, Bury and Derby County before joining Wednesday from Southampton for £100,000 in March 1979. He was an immediate success at Hillsborough, ending the 1979–80 season as the club's top scorer with 22 goals in 41 league games to help Wednesday win promotion to the second division. When the Owls just missed out on promotion to the top flight in 1981–82, Curran decided he wanted to leave and negotiated his own transfer to Sheffield United. He played in just 33 league games for the Blades before being sold to Everton for a larger fee than the tribunal had set when he moved across the city. At Goodison Park, he made just enough appearances to qualify for a league championship medal in 1984–85, but left to play for Huddersfield Town. He later played for Hull City, Sunderland and Grimsby Town, ending his league career with Chesterfield.

CURTIS, NORMAN. Left-back Norman Curtis joined Wednesday from Gainsborough Trinity in January 1950 and made his debut towards the end of the year in a 4–3 home defeat by Bolton Wanderers. He won a regular place in the side midway through the following season, helping Wednesday win the second division championship. In 1952–53, he was an ever-present, scoring six goals from the penalty spot, including two against both Derby County and Portsmouth. His technique was unusual to say the least – a colleague would place the ball on the spot and Curtis would charge at full speed from his own half of the pitch before blasting the ball past a terrified goalkeeper. Curtis also saved two penalties in the match against Preston

North End when McIntosh had to go off after being injured. Nicknamed 'Cannonball', the Dinnington-born defender was an ever-present when Wednesday won the second division title in 1958–59, but after losing his place to Don Megson, he joined Doncaster Rovers as player-manager.

D

DAILEY, JIMMY. Scottish-born Jimmy Dailey began his career as an amateur with Wolverhampton Wanderers during the early part of the Second World War but was later allowed to return north of the border, where he signed for Third Lanark. He joined Sheffield Wednesday in November 1946 and scored the Owls' second goal in a 2–2 draw at home to West Bromwich Albion. That season he scored 13 goals in 17 league appearances including a hat-trick in a 5–1 win over Tottenham Hotspur. The following season he scored all five goals as Barnsley were hammered 5–2 at Hillsborough. However, despite that goalscoring achievement, he failed to command a regular place and in 1949 was allowed to join Birmingham City for £9,500. A great favourite with the Wednesday fans, he scored 25 goals in just 41 appearances, a goal ratio he kept up at St Andrews and later with Exeter, Workington and Rochdale, ending his career with 161 goals in 346 league appearances.

DAVIS, HARRY. The first Harry Davis to play for Wednesday was signed from Football Alliance side Birmingham St Georges in 1892, in time to play in the club's first game in the Football League. The club already knew of his ability for he had led the Alliance attack in the match against the Football League at Olive Grove in 1891, scoring a goal. Some records name Davis as the scorer of the club's first League goal at Notts County. He did score some memorable goals in his time at Wednesday and hit a hat-trick in a 6–1 FA Cup win over Middlesbrough in February 1895. He left the club at the end of the Olive Grove era after helping Wednesday win the FA Cup for the first time in 1896.

DAVIS, HARRY. Arriving at Owlerton from Barnsley in 1900, Davis helped the club to promotion and settled in well, forming an effective right-wing partnership with Harry Chapman. At 5 ft 4in, he was one of the smallest players in the first division. In 1902–03, he scored 13 league goals as Wednesday won the league title, including a hat-trick in a 3–0 home win over Bolton Wanderers. His form that season led to him winning the first of three caps for England, scoring in a 4–0 win over Ireland at Molineux. Having contributed greatly to the club's FA Cup runs of 1904 and 1905 when they lost on each occasion at the semi-final stage, he missed Wednesday's 2–1 win over Everton in the 1907 final having broken his leg in the third-round replay at Sunderland. The injury ended his playing career and he became the club's assistant-trainer, a position he held for many years.

DAVISON, TEDDY. The smallest goalkeeper ever to play for England, Teddy Davison joined Wednesday from Gateshead in 1908 after impressing in a trial game and saving a penalty. He was renowned for saving penalty kicks and on a number of occasions, saved two in a game. He made his debut for Wednesday in a 2–0 home win over Bristol City and over the next 18 years played in 424 league and Cup games. Though honours at club level eluded Davison, he played for the Sheffield FA and in 1925 toured Australia with the FA, playing in 13 games. In 1922, he won his one and only cap for England in their 1–0 win against Wales at Liverpool. His last game for Wednesday was at Hull City just before Christmas 1924, when the Tigers beat the Owls 4–2. After a short spell as Mansfield Town's player–manager, he began the first of two spells as secretary–manager of Chesterfield. He later managed Sheffield United from 1932 until 1952, taking the Blades to the FA Cup final in 1936 and missing out on promotion in 1937–38 on goal average.

DEBUTS. The only player to score a hat-trick on his league debut for Sheffield Wednesday is Ted Harper. Signed from Blackburn Rovers, he made his debut on 26 November 1927 against Derby County at the Baseball Ground. His hat-trick came in a 6–4 win for the Owls.

DEFEATS – FEWEST. During the 1899–1900 season, Sheffield Wednesday went through the 34 match programme and suffered only five defeats as they won the second division championship. In recent years, Wednesday lost six matches of the 42 played in 1983–84 as they finished runners-up on goal average to Chelsea in the Second Division.

DEFEATS – MOST. A total of 26 defeats, suffered during the 1919–20 and 1974–75 seasons, is the worst in the club's history. Not surprisingly, on both occasions they finished bottom (of division one in 1919–20 and division two in 1974–75) and were relegated.

DEFEATS – WORST. Sheffield Wednesday's record defeat was when Aston Villa beat them 10–0 at Villa Park on 5 October 1912. Despite this result, Wednesday finished third in the first division with Villa in second place. The club have had nine goals put past them on two occasions: 9–0 at Derby County in 1898–99 and 9–3 at Everton in 1931–32. Wednesday's worst home defeat is 7–1 by Nottingham Forest during the 1994–95 season.

DEFENSIVE RECORDS. Sheffield Wednesday's best defensive record was established in 1899–1900 when the club won the second division championship. They conceded just 22 goals in that campaign of 34 matches, losing on five occasions. The club's best defensive record over a 42 match programme came in 1983–84 when they conceded 34 goals in finishing second to Chelsea in division two. Wednesday's worst defensive record was in 1954–55 when they let in 100 goals to finish bottom of the first division.

DEGRYSE, MARC. The Belgian international midfielder, who has won over 60 caps for his country, joined Sheffield Wednesday from Anderlecht for £1.5 million in August 1995. An instant hit with the Wednesday fans, his neat control and thoughtful distribution stood out in what was a disappointing season for the Owls. He scored some very important goals for the club, including a first-minute winner at Southampton and the only goal of the game against high-flying Arsenal. For that match, a party of fans from Belgium came over at Easter to watch the popular international.

DERBIES. The tradition of dourness and close-fought contests in the Sheffield derby stems from the early games between the teams in the period up to the First World War. The teams had met several times prior to the first league game on 16 October 1893 which ended in a 1–1 draw, and there was already bad feeling between the two clubs. One of the bones of contention was that several players had left Wednesday for United when the Blades were formed in 1890. The return game in that 1893–94 season was at Olive Grove, Wednesday's first permanent ground, but United won 2–1 after Brandon missed a penalty for the Owls. Sheffield Wednesday did not record their first victory until 7 September 1895 when a goal by Bell separated the teams. Their first league victory at Bramall Lane did not come until the first match of the 1902–03 season when they won 3–2. The two clubs first met in the FA Cup competition in February 1900. The match at Bramall Lane was abandoned after 50 minutes because of a snowstorm. The replay a week later ended at 1–1, but proved to be a bad-tempered affair with Massey, Millar and Spiksley all picking up injuries and missing the Owlerton replay on 19 February. That game was one of the most ferocious battles in the history of the Sheffield derby. After 38 minutes, Wednesday's Lee was carried off with a broken leg and three minutes into the second half, Ambrose Langley conceded the penalty from which Ernest Needham gave United the lead. Wednesday's Pryce put Hedley out of the game with a deliberate kick and was immediately sent off, as was Langley who ended Walter Bennett's interest in the match. Billy Beers added a second goal for United against a Wednesday side reduced to eight men. One of the great derby games of this period was the 3–3 draw at Bramall Lane on 6 November 1909. United went 2–0 up in the first twenty minutes before two goals fom Sammy Kirkman and another by Harry Chapman gave Wednesday the lead. Only ten minutes remained when Simmons dived in to meet Evans's centre from the left to send the 30,000 crowd home happy. In the five seasons up to the intervention of the First World War, Wednesday won seven times with three draws, although in the last two of these seasons, the Blades finished higher in the League. The 1913–14 games were both won by the Owls, helping them retain their first division status. Although they finished only three points behind United, who were tenth, Wednesday were just one place and four points clear of relegation. Wednesday's biggest league win in the derby match came on 22 September 1928 when they beat United 5–2. United scored five goals on 3 March 1934 when Billy Boyd hit a hat-trick in a 5–1 win. The 1937–38 season marked the first Wednesday v United games in division two, with the Bramall Lane side winning both games. The game at Bramall Lane the following season was goalless, the first time either side had failed to score in 90 minutes of football, though there had been 19 drawn games. On 8 September 1951, United beat Wednesday 7–3 in a game full of incident. Thomas scored what was to be his only first-team goal for Wednesday with a diving header in the second minute. United equalised through Ringstead and then went ahead after 20 minutes through Harold Brook. Owls' keeper Dave McIntosh then saved a Fred Furniss penalty before Wednesday drew level on the hour when Woodhead netted from close range. He later scored a third for Wednesday but the Hillsborough side were completely overrun in the last half-hour with two goals from Haksworth and one each from Brook, Ringstead and Smith. The Boxing Day fixture at Hillsborough in 1979 attracted a record third-division crowd of 49,309. The match kicked off at 11.00 a.m. but such was the excitement that very few spectators missed the early start. Wednesday won 4–0 with goals from Mellor, Curran, King and Mark Smith. On 3 April 1993, the two clubs met at Wembley in the semi-final of the FA Cup in front of a 75,364 crowd. Despite the old warhorse Alan Cork conjuring a goal out of nothing, goals from Mark Bright and Chris Waddle ensured it was Wednesday who enjoyed their day out at the final in May.

Sheffield Wednesday's record v Sheffield United

	P	W	D	L	F	A
Premier League	4	1	3	0	6	4
First Division	80	26	24	30	105	114

Second Division	12	3	2	7	11	20
Third Division	2	1	1	0	5	1
FA Cup	10	3	4	3	13	14
League Cup	2	1	1	0	3	1
Total	110	35	35	40	143	154

DEWAR, NEIL. Billy Walker's first signing, Neil Dewar, began his career with Third Lanark where he scored 124 goals and helped them win the Scottish league second division title in 1930–31. The following season he made his debut for Scotland and after impressing in the match against England at Wembley, he scored a hat-trick against France in Paris. This prompted Manchester United to sign him in February 1933 for £6,000 but he never really settled at Old Trafford and after scoring 14 goals in 34 games, he joined Sheffield Wednesday. The tall centre-forward made his debut in a 1–1 draw at home to Manchester City in December 1933 and though

Neil Dewar

he lost his place the following season to Jack Palethorpe, he bounced back in 1935–36 to score 21 goals in 36 league and Cup appearances. During his last season at Hillsborough, he scored his second hat-trick for the club in a 6–4 win over Everton and when he played his last game for the Owls on the final day of the 1936–37 season, he had scored 50 goals in 97 league and Cup games for Wednesday. Dewar also scored the only goal of the 1935 FA Charity Shield against Arsenal.

DISASTER. The worst disaster in the history of British football took place at the home of Sheffield Wednesday on 15 April 1989 and resulted in the deaths of 95 people and a further 170 injuries. That year, Hillsborough was the venue for the FA Cup semi-final between Liverpool and Nottingham Forest and a large crowd arrived to see the match. The Leppings Lane End of the ground was full of Liverpool fans, and spectators at the front of the overcrowded area were crushed against the perimeter fencing which was meant to prevent pitch invasions. Even police horses were lifted from the ground by the force of the fans in the confusion that followed. No one quite realised that a major disaster was taking place. Just six minutes of the match had been played when it was abandoned. The entire footballing world was stunned by the enormity of the tragedy, which was seen by a television audience of millions.

DISMISSALS. Playing for Sheffield Wednesday against Lincoln in 1888, Tom Cawley, who had an exemplary disciplinary record was sent off in error. Realising his mistake almost immediately, the official called Cawley back, but the player refused to return on a matter of principle. The second-round FA Cup replay between Wednesday and Sheffield United on 19 February 1900 turned into something of a battle when the Owls lost Lee with a broken leg after 38 minutes. The Blades finished the game with nine men after losing Hedley and Bennett injured and Wednesday with eight following the sendings-off of Pryce and Langley, both dismissed for deliberate kicks on the two United players stretchered from the field. The match was described as a disgrace – 'a game of wild excitement which sadly tarnished the image of Sheffield football'. The result was a 2–0 win for Sheffield United. In more recent times, Nigel Worthington had the unenviable record of being the first Sheffield Wednesday player to be dismissed in a Premier League game, when he got his marching orders against Liverpool at Hillsborough on 27 February 1993.

DOBSON, COLIN. Discovered playing amateur football in the north east, the Middlesbrough-born forward insisted on completing his shipbuilding apprenticeship and so, despite being on Wednesday's books for almost five years, he didn't make his debut until September 1961. Playing at either inside-forward or on the left-wing, he impressed so much that by 1963 he had made two appearances for the England Under-23 side against Yugoslavia and Romania. An ever-present during 1964–65, he lost his place towards the end of the following season as manager Alan Brown made some tactical changes, and so missed the chance of

45

appearing in the FA Cup final. He had scored 52 goals in 193 first-team appearances for the Owls when he joined Huddersfield Town in August 1966 where he also scored a half-century of goals.

DOOLEY, DEREK. Big and ungainly, Derek Dooley's sensational goalscoring exploits of 1951–52 made him a folk hero. He joined Wednesday in 1947 after a spell as an amateur with Lincoln City but his first two outings in the first team were disappointing and it wasn't until he got his third chance against Barnsley in October 1951 that he began to show what he could do. He scored both Wednesday's goals that day in a 2–1 win. Two games later, he embarked on a scoring run, finding the net in nine consecutive league games. The run included five goals in a 6–0 win over Notts County, all four in a 4–0 victory over Everton and a hat-trick in a 6–0 win at West Ham United. He finished the season with 46 goals in the League as the Owls lifted the second division title. In 1952–53, he found life a little harder in top-flight football but worked at his game and had just rediscovered his scoring touch

Derek Dooley

with 16 goals in 29 games when tragedy struck. At Preston North End in February 1953, Dooley broke his leg in a collision with goalkeeper George Thompson. The limb became infected with gangrene and had to be amputated to save his life. His benefit game at Hillsborough in 1955 was the club's first under their new floodlights and raised £15,000. In 1962, he took charge of the club's new Development Fund and stayed in the post until he was appointed Wednesday's team manager in 1971. A reflective, pipe-smoking man, he steered the team to the top of the second division early in 1972–73, but then results fell away. The following season, the team appeared to have turned the corner, but on Christmas Eve, Dooley was sacked. He switched his allegiance to Sheffield United, working as commercial manager, director and managing director.

DRAWS. Sheffield Wednesday played their greatest number of drawn league matches in a single season in 1978–79 when 19 of their matches ended all-square, and their fewest in their first season in the League, 1892–93, when only three of their matches were drawn. The club's highest scoring draw is 5–5, at home to Everton in the first division on 12 November 1904.

E

EARLY GROUNDS. Though the club played many of its major matches at Bramall Lane, Wednesday's first ground for regular games was south of Bramall Lane on London Road, where Highfields Library now stands. Within a couple of years they had moved to the Ball Inn ground, Myrtle Road, which is now a sports centre. In 1877 they hired the Sheaf House cricket ground. Other games were played occasionally at Hunters Bar. After turning professional in 1887 and having to meet players' wages, the club decided they could no longer pay a share of the gate receipts for their more important matches at Sheaf House or Bramall Lane and so they opted to acquire a ground of their own. This they did by leasing Olive Grove from the Duke of Norfolk.

EARP, JACK. Captain of the first Wednesday team to win the FA Cup in 1896, Jack Earp arrived at the club after two spells with Nottingham Forest and a short stay at Everton. Forming an outstanding full-back partnership with Ambrose Langley, he made his Wednesday debut at Stoke in October 1893. A man of strong principle, Earp preferred not to play football on Christmas Day, although he did play at Bolton in his first season with the club. In 1898 he represented the Football League against the Irish League but in 1900 after playing in 174 league and Cup games for the club, he left to join Stockport.

48

EIRE. The first Sheffield Wednesday player to be capped by the Republic of Ireland was Bill Fallon when he played against Hungary in 1939. The most capped player in the Owls history is John Sheridan who won 27 caps playing for his country whilst at Hillsborough.

ELLIS, KEITH. Though he made his debut in the 2–0 win over Preston North End in March 1955, Keith Ellis's opportunities over the next four seasons were limited due to the fine form of Roy Shiner. In 1955–56 he did not play at all and in 1956–57 he played in just six games, though he did score a hat-trick in the 3–1 defeat of Birmingham City on the last day of the season. It was only when Harry Catterick was manager that Ellis was given a proper chance and in 1960–61, he scored 19 goals in 37 first-team appearances, including a hat-trick in the 7–2 win at Old Trafford against Manchester United. Following the arrival of Vic Buckingham as manager, Ellis fell out of favour, though he did score Wednesday's first-ever goal in European football in the 4–2 defeat at Olympique Lyonnais. In March 1964, he joined Scunthorpe United for £10,000, later playing for Cardiff City and Lincoln City before hanging up his boots.

ELLIS, SAM. After playing in just ten League games, teenaged centre-half Sam Ellis made his FA Cup debut at Wembley in the 1966 final against Everton. Occasionally looking rather awkward, Ellis established himself as a regular in the first team until he had a spell out of favour towards the end of the 1967–68 season. He bounced back and represented England at Under-23 level on three occasions. In January 1972, after appearing in 181 games for the Owls, he joined former Wednesday boss Danny Williams at Mansfield Town.

Sam Ellis

He later played in 173 league games for Lincoln City, scoring 33 goals before following Graham Taylor to Watford, where he ended his league career and became the club coach. In the summer of 1982 he became manager of Blackpool and after having had to apply for re-election at the end of his first season in charge, led the Seasiders to promotion two years later. In May 1989, he took over at Bury, but after the Shakers lost out in the third division play-offs, he moved to Maine Road to become Peter Reid's assistant.

EURO '96. Hillsborough staged the following matches in Euro '96.

Denmark	1	Portugal	1
Croatia	3	Denmark	0
Turkey	0	Denmark	3

EUSTACE, PETER. Although he made his Wednesday debut in August 1962, it was another two years before he became an established member of the first team. He played exceptionally well in the Owls' run to the 1966 FA Cup final. Tall and elegant, Eustace was initially a wing-half, but later became a midfield player with plenty of flare. He gave a particularly memorable performance in Wednesday's 3–1 third-round FA Cup replay win at Leeds United in January 1969. Wednesday manager Danny Williams raved over Eustace's performances, saying he was the best player he had ever had. Yet in January 1970, he sold him to West Ham United for £90,000. Eustace was unable to reproduce his form at Upton Park and after a short loan spell at Rotherham United he was taken back to Hillsborough by Derek Dooley for a much-reduced fee. He played the last of his 280 first-team games against Millwall in March 1974 before joining Peterborough United. He took on the job of coach at Sunderland but in 1983 Howard Wilkinson made him assistant at Hillsborough. In October 1988, he took charge

Peter Eustace

following Wilkinson's move to Leeds, but after the club won only two games in 19 matches, he was sacked. In July 1991 he took over from Frank Clark as Leyton Orient team manager, assuming full control after Clark's departure to Nottingham Forest, but left the club in 1994.

EVER-PRESENTS. There have been 54 Sheffield Wednesday players who have been ever present throughout a league season. The greatest number of ever-present seasons by a Wednesday player is four by Don Megson and Martin Hodge.

EVERTON. Sheffield Wednesday and Everton have been drawn together more times in the FA Cup than any other pair of clubs in history. They have clashed in 16 ties, including two finals in 1907 and 1966. Wednesday have won three and Everton eight, whilst five have been drawn. The two clubs have also produced some exciting scorelines in league encounters. Wednesday won the first-ever meeting at Goodison Park 5–3, whilst Everton gained revenge the following season with a resounding 8–1 victory. On 12 November 1904, the clubs played out a 5–5 draw, the highest in Wednesday's history. On Christmas Day 1929, Mark Hooper scored a hat-trick in a 4–1 win at Goodison Park, whilst in the Boxing Day return at Hillsborough, Wednesday won 4–0 to complete the double. Another high-scoring match between the two clubs came on 10 September 1936, when Neil Dewar hit a hat-trick in a 6–4 win for Wednesday.

F

FA CUP. Sheffield Wednesday first participated in the FA Cup in December 1880 and caused a great sensation by travelling across the Pennines and beating the mighty Blackburn Rovers 4–0 with Bob Gregory grabbing a hat-trick. Since then they have gone on to win the trophy on three occasions. Their first appearance in a final was in 1890 when they lost 6–1 against Blackburn Rovers at the Kennington Oval.

FOOTBALL · SHEFFIELD WEDNESDAY

The 1935 FA Cup winners

FA CUP FINALS. Sheffield Wednesday have appeared in six FA Cup finals, winning the trophy on three occasions:

1890 v Blackburn Rovers (Kennington Oval)	1–6	
1896 v Wolverhampton Wanderers (Crystal Palace)	2–1	
1907 v Everton (Crystal Palace)	2–1	
1935 v West Bromwich Albion (Wembley)	4–2	
1966 v Everton (Wembley)	2–3	
1993 v Arsenal (Wembley)	1–2	

aet after 1–1 draw

FA CUP SEMI-FINALS. Sheffield Wednesday have participated in 14 FA Cup semi-finals up to the end of the 1996–97 season.

FANS. When Wednesday were relegated to the third division for the first time in the club's history in 1975, it really shook the fans. One of the most bitter was Ken Wood; unable to face the prospect of seeing the Owls in the lower reaches of the League, he tore up his rosette, burnt his scarf and gave away his rattle before announcing his decision to emigrate. Another disgruntled Wednesday fan was Bob Montgomery who attempted, albeit unsuccessfully, to take the club to court for their uninspiring performance in an FA Cup replay against Southend United in 1983. His argument was that the game Wednesday played had been so bad, it was not football at all and thus an offence under the Trades Descriptions Act, the club having obtained his entrance money (which he now demanded be given back to him) under false pretences.

FANTHAM, JOHN. The holder of Sheffield Wednesday's post-war aggregate scoring record, John Fantham made his first-team debut in a 2–0 win over Tottenham Hotspur in February 1958. However, it was only when Albert Quixall left Hillsborough to join Manchester United at the start of the following season that Fantham came into his own. In his first full season, he won a second division championship medal and in 1959–60, topped the Wednesday scoring charts for the first of what was to be five occasions. His best season in terms of goals scored was 1961–62, when he netted 24 times, including scoring his first hat-trick for the club in the 5–1 defeat of Birmingham City. He notched two other hat-tricks in his Wednesday career: at home to Burnley (in

1964–65) (5–1) and at home to Southampton (in 1966–67) (4–1). His achievements were recognised in the early 1960s when he won FA, Under-23 and football league honours and there is no doubt that he deserved more than the one England cap he was awarded in 1961 when he played against Luxembourg. Fantham scored 167 goals in 435 league and Cup appearances for the Owls before manager Danny Williams opted to sell the ace marksman to Rotherham United for £5,000 in October 1969. He went on to appear in 51 league games for the Millmoor club before retiring to become a successful businessman.

FATHER AND SON. Sheffield Wednesday have boasted a number of father and son players, the most notable being the Froggatts and the Megsons. Frank Froggatt, who played in 95 first-team games for the Owls did not see his son Redfern enjoy his great success with the club, dying in 1942 when his offspring was only 18. Redfern went on to win four England caps and scored 149 goals in 458 appearances for Wednesday. Don Megson captained the Owls to the FA Cup final in 1966 and represented the Football League against the Italian League. He played in 442 games for the Hillsborough club, seemingly enjoying each and every one. His son Gary, currently manager of Stockport County was instrumental in the Owls winning promotion to the first division in 1983–84, when he was an ever-present.

FELTON, BILLY. Jarrow-born Billy Felton joined Wednesday on New Year's Day 1923 in rather unusual circumstances. He was about to travel with his Grimsby Town team-mates to Accrington, when he was told of the Sheffield club's interest in him. He left the train and signed for the Owls there and then. That afternoon he made his debut for the club in the goalless draw against Southampton at Hillsborough. A strong-tackling right-back with good powers of recovery, he and Ernest Blenkinsop formed one of the best full-back pairings outside of the first division. His consistency earned him an England cap against France in Paris in 1925. However, towards the end of the following season, he lost his place and only played in odd games as a replacement for Blenkinsop or Tommy Walker, who had joined the club from Bradford City. In March 1929 he joined Manchester City before moving to White Hart Lane, where he made 75 first-team appearances for Spurs, captaining them to promotion from the second division in 1933.

FERRIER, BOB. Signed from Dunfermline in 1894, inside-forward Bob Ferrier made his Wednesday debut in the opening game of the 1894–95 season at Everton. The Toffees were again Wednesday's opponents in the quarter-final of the FA Cup when a badly injured Ferrier cut in from the wing to score the second goal in a 2–0 win. Unfortunately, Ferrier's injury meant he missed the semi-final and, in fact, he did not play again until the following season. In 1898, he switched from inside-forward to wing-half and the following season, helped the club win the second division championship. In 1900–01 he was the only ever-present as Wednesday finished eighth in their first season in the top flight following promotion. Ferrier was an important member of the Wednesday side that won the first division championship in 1902–03 and 1903–04, missing just four games over the two campaigns. He had played in 329 games for Wednesday when he lost his place to Ruddlesdin and returned to live in Scotland, where his Sheffield-born son later starred for Motherwell.

FEWEST DEFEATS. During Sheffield Wednesday's second division championship winning season of 1899–1900, the club went through the 34 match programme losing only five games. The first of these came in the 15th game of the season at Chesterfield (0–1) after the club had won 11 and drawn three of the first 14 fixtures. They lost three other games at Bolton Wanderers, Newton Heath and Barnsley, all by the same scoreline of 0–1, and lost 4–1 at Small Heath. This was the season when the club won all 17 of its home fixtures.

FINNEY, ALAN. The Langwith-born winger was just 17 years old when he made his debut for Wednesday in a 2–2 draw at home to Chelsea in February 1951. His first goal for the club came in the final game of that season as the Owls beat Spurs 6–0. Finney scored a number of memorable goals in his 16 seasons with the club; his only hat-trick was also against Spurs when Wednesday won 4–1 at Hillsborough on 17 November 1956. Finney won three second division championship medals with the club in 1951–52, 1955–56

55

and 1958–59 and was an ever-present in 1960–61 when the Owls finished runners-up in the first division. He gained international recognition for England at B and Under-23 level but never the full cap that his play deserved. Able to play on either flank, Finney was often criticised for not scoring more goals. Yet in 503 first-team appearances for the Owls, he not only netted 90 goals but made many more for his team-mates. He left Hillsborough in January 1966 to join Doncaster Rovers, hanging up his boots after appearing in 30 league games for the Belle Vue club.

FIRST DIVISION. Sheffield Wednesday have had nine spells in the first division. Elected to the enlarged league division one in 1892, the Owls spent seven seasons in the top flight before suffering relegation in 1898–99. Promoted immediately, Wednesday then had their longest spell in the first division, winning the league championship twice during the 16 seasons before relegation in 1919–20. After winning the second division championship in 1925–26, Wednesday spent 11 seasons in division one, winning the league championship in 1928–29 and 1929–30 and finishing third on four occasions. After relegation in 1936–37, the Owls didn't return to the first division until 1950–51, but after a disastrous season, they went straight back down to the second division. The 1951–52 season was a complete contrast as Wednesday won the division two title to return for a fifth spell in the first division. The club lasted three seasons, struggling in each one, before being relegated in 1954–55. Again the Owls won the second division championship at the first time of asking but after a mediocre season in 1956–57, were relegated the next. As on the previous two occasions, Wednesday won the second division championship to make an immediate return to the top flight. The Owls then spent 11 seasons in the first division, finishing as runners-up to Tottenham Hotspur during the London club's double-winning season of 1960–61. After relegation to the second division in 1969–70, the club dropped into the third division before eventually returning to division one in 1984–85. After six seasons, Wednesday were relegated but won promotion in their first season in division two. The club then spent the 1991–92 season in the first division before the Premier League took over.

FIRST LEAGUE MATCH. After gaining admission to the Football League in May 1892, being elected to the enlarged first division, Wednesday played their first match at Notts County's Castle Ground on 3 September. In a fairly drab encounter, Wednesday won 1–0 with captain Tom Brandon being credited with the goal, although some records give it to Harry Davis, the Smethwick-born forward from Birmingham St George. The Wednesday side was: W. Allan; T. Brandon; A. Mumford; A. Hall; W. Betts; H. Brandon; F. Spiksley; A. Brady; H. Davis; R. Brown and W. Dunlop.

FIRST MATCH. Wednesday's first game was played on 31 December 1867 against Dronfield. Wednesday won 1–0, although Dronfield scored four 'rogues', that is to say they put the ball through an outer goal four times. Wednesday, however, got the ball through the inner goal, which was worth any number of rogues. The identity of the scorer of Wednesday's goal has never been established.

FLOODLIGHTS. Hillsborough switched on its floodlights for the first time on 9 March 1955 when a Sheffield XI played an International XI in aid of Derek Dooley who had recently lost a leg following a playing accident. A crowd of 55,000 paid £7,500 to see the International XI win 5–1. Regarded at the time as the most advanced installation to date, the floodlights were mounted on six square-shaped pylons. Not long after, a Football League v Scottish League game was played under the new lights, followed by a series of floodlit friendlies with foreign opposition. The first league match to be played under lights was on 21 March 1956 when Wednesday beat Barnsley 3–0 in front of a 31,577 crowd.

FLU EPIDEMIC. A flu epidemic at Hillsborough caused Wednesday to start the 1957–58 season a week late. They never seemed to recover, not winning a single away game, and finished bottom of the first division.

FOOTBALL ALLIANCE. Founder members of this competition, Wednesday spent three seasons in the Football Alliance prior to their election to the Football League in 1892. In their first season in 1889–90, Wednesday won the Alliance, scoring 70 goals in the process. They beat Long Eaton and Small Heath at Olive Grove by the score of 9–1 and won all of their 11 home matches in the competition. In a remarkable turnaround, Wednesday finished bottom of the Alliance in their second season in the competition, failing to win any of their eleven away fixtures. In the club's final season in the competition, they finished fourth. Wednesday's overall record in the Alliance was:

P	W	D	L	F	A	Pts
66	31	11	24	175	140	73

FOOTBALLER OF THE YEAR. Only one Sheffield Wednesday player has been honoured by the Football Writers' Association as their choice for Player of the Year – Chris Waddle in 1992–93.

FOOTBALL LEAGUE CUP. Sheffield Wednesday were one of five clubs that shunned the first tournament, not entering until 1966–67 when they went out of the competition at the first hurdle, losing 1–0 at home to Rotherham United. Sad to relate, the Owls, with the exception of the last few years, have failed to make much impact upon the League (later Milk, Littlewoods, Rumbelows and Coca-Cola) Cup. In 1973–74, Wednesday lost 8–2 in a third-round tie at Queens Park Rangers and two seasons later, lost on penalties against Darlington. The club's first hat-trick in the competition was scored by Rodger Wylde in a 5–2 win over Doncaster Rovers on 13 August 1977. In 1986–87, Stockport County were beaten 10–0 on aggregate, with Colin Walker netting a hat-trick in a 7–0 second-leg win at Edgeley Park. When Wednesday won 8–0 at Aldershot in a second-round second-leg tie on 3 October 1989, it established a new record away win for the competition. In 1990–91, Sheffield Wednesday won the trophy for the first time in their history. They began none too surely against third division Brentford, needing two second-half goals to overturn a deficit in the opening 45 minutes in the home leg, but repeated the scoreline at Griffin Park. The Owls were again showing signs of nerves in being held to a goalless draw by Swindon Town at Hillsborough, but managed a 1–0 win at the County Ground. Wednesday then had to settle for a 1–1 draw at home to Derby County before winning the replay 2–1. In the fifth round, a Nigel Pearson goal gave them a 1–0 victory at Coventry City. In the semi-final, the Owls won well at Stamford Bridge,

2–0, and equally effectively 3–1 at Hillsborough. In the final, Wednesday beat Manchester United 1–0, with their goal coming from a fine shot driven in by John Sheridan from the edge of the penalty area after 37 minutes. Wednesday reached the final again in 1992–93. After defeating Hartlepool United 5–2 on aggregate, the Owls thrashed Leicester City 7–1 and Queens Park Rangers 4–0 before needing a replay to beat Ipswich Town. In the semi-final, Wednesday punished a lethargic Blackburn Rovers side with a 4–2 victory at Ewood Park with Warhurst deputising admirably for the injured Hirst. In the final, they faced Arsenal and stole the lead through John Harkes after Paul Warhurst had hit the post after five minutes. But goals from Merson and Morrow provided the Gunners with an unlikely victory. The following season, Bolton, Middlesbrough and Queens Park Rangers were beaten in the first three rounds before a stirring performance against Wimbledon at Selhurst Park took the Owls through to the semi-final against Manchester United. The club's challenge ended here with defeats in both legs, 1–0 at Old Trafford and 4–1 at Hillsborough.

FORD, DAVID. When David Ford made his debut against Sunderland on 23 October 1965, he became the first substitute the club had ever used in league football. At the end of the season, he was playing in the FA Cup final at Wembley, scoring one of the goals in Wednesday's 3–2 defeat. He won the first of his two England Under-23 caps in 1966 when he played against Wales and in 1966–67 he top scored for the Owls with 14 league goals, including a hat-trick in a 7–0 win over Burnley. Around this time, the Wednesday forward was involved in a car crash and it took a little while for him to recover. Having lost some of his speed, he was allowed to join Newcastle United in a deal which brought Jackie Sinclair to Hillsborough. After just over 12 months at St James's Park, Ford returned to Sheffield, but this time to United, helping the Blades win promotion in 1970–71. In the summer of 1973 he moved to Halifax Town, playing in almost 100 games for the Shaymen before retiring.

FORMATION. Sheffield Wednesday Football Club came into being on the evening of 4 September 1867 when the Wednesday Cricket Club (founded in 1820) formed a football section. The name 'Wednesday' had been adopted by the cricketers for the simple reason that that was the weekday afternoon when they took time off work to play sport. The meeting to form the football section of the club was held at the Adelphi pub, a building eventually demolished to make way for the Crucible Theatre, scene of many recent sporting dramas in the world snooker championships. Wednesday became the city's leading club within ten years of its formation, having dominated local Cup football almost since its foundation.

FRANCIS, TREVOR. Plymouth-born Trevor Francis made his name with Birmingham City in the early 1970s. On 20 February 1971, he became the first 16 year old to score four goals in a league game, when Bolton were beaten 4–0 at St Andrews. After 280 league games for Birmingham City in which he scored 118 goals, he became Britain's first seven-figure signing when Nottingham Forest paid a reported £1.5 million for his services in February 1979. Despite being plagued by injuries at the City Ground, he scored the winning goal in the 1979 European Cup final against Malmo FF. Just one week into the 1981–82 season, he joined Manchester City. A year later he was on his way to Sampdoria, where he won an Italian Cup winners' medal. After a spell with Atlanta, he signed for Glasgow Rangers. A Skol Cup winners' medal at Ibrox was followed by a return to league football with Queens Park Rangers. After a year as player–manager at Loftus Road, he took up a similar position with Sheffield Wednesday in June 1991, having joined the club as a player in January 1990. Unlucky to be relegated in 1989–90, Wednesday bounced back immediately the following season after finishing third, and won the League Cup, though Francis was a non-playing substitute that day. After Atkinson's departure, Francis took over the reins and in his first season, the Owls finished third in the first division. In 1992–93, Francis took the club to two domestic finals, but there was nothing to show for all their efforts but losers' medals. In 1993–94, Wednesday finished seventh in the Premier League, as they had the previous season. Despite being busy in the close-season transfer market, the Owls could only finish the 1994–95 season in mid-table and in May 1995, Francis was dismissed. He is now back at his beloved St Andrews as manager of Birmingham City.

Trevor Francis

FRIENDLIES. In December 1934, Wednesday played the famous Austria FC at Hillsborough and a crowd of 12,445 saw the Owls end the visitors' unbeaten tour run. They won 3–0, with two goals from Ellis Rimmer and one from Walter Millership. After the installation of floodlights, Wednesday arranged a number of friendly matches against foreign opposition. In October 1955, they went down 7–1 to Hungarian side Vasas Budapest but in January 1956, hat-tricks from Roy Shiner and Alan Finney helped the Owls beat San Lorenzo 9–0. On 22 October 1962, Brazilian champions Santos, complete with Pelé, visited Hillsborough. A crowd of 49,058 saw the South American side win 4–2 with the legendary Brazilian beating Ron Springett with a remarkable penalty kick.

FROGGATT, FRANK. A determined, hard-tackling defender, Frank Froggatt was signed from Denaby United in late 1921 and made his debut in the 2–1 win over Bradford in October. For the first four seasons of his Wednesday career, he was forced to live in the shadow of the club's England international, George Wilson. However, in 1925–26, he came into his own and was appointed club captain. An ever-present during that campaign, he led the Owls to the second division championship – a feat that his son Redfern repeated in 1958–59. At the beginning of the following season, he scored his only goal for the club in a 5–3 defeat at Leicester City but when Fred Kean was made centre-half, he lost his place and the captaincy. In 1927–28, he moved to Notts County and later played with Chesterfield but unfortunately he did not live to see his son Redfern enjoy success with the Owls, dying in 1942.

Frank Froggatt

FROGGATT, REDFERN. After making his Wednesday debut in the League Cup (North) match against Grimsby Town, Redfern Froggatt played in 86 wartime matches before making his League debut in the opening game of the 1946–47 season. A clever inside-forward who scored more than his share of goals, he was chosen for England B against Switzerland in 1950 before winning his first full cap against Wales at Wembley in 1952. Froggatt won four full caps for England; against Scotland in 1953, he formed a left-wing partnership with his cousin, Portsmouth's Jack Froggatt. Froggatt established a post-war scoring record and helped the Owls win promotion four times, collecting three second division championship medals in the process. His best season in terms of goals scored was 1958–59 when he netted 26 in 37 league appearances, including a hat-trick in a 6–0 win over Sunderland. That season, he followed in his father Frank's footsteps by captaining the side to the second division title. He played the last of his 458 League and Cup games against West Ham United on the final day of the 1959–60 season, having scored 149 goals.

FULL MEMBERS CUP. Wednesday's only match in this competition came on 25 November 1986 when a crowd of 7,846 saw the Owls lose 1–0 at Hillsborough against second division Portsmouth.

G

GANNON, EDDIE. Dublin-born Eddie Gannon was signed from Notts County by Eric Taylor in March 1949 for £15,000, after he had made 106 league appearances for the Meadow Lane club. Although he scored very few goals himself, his attacking wing-half play made many for his colleagues. Making his debut for the Republic of Ireland against Belgium in 1949, he went on to win 11 caps. His most successful seasons at the club were 1949–50 and 1951–52 when the club won promotion, yet in 1953–54 he was at his peak in Wednesday's run to the FA Cup semi-final. After playing in 219 first-team games, he left the club in 1955 to become player–manager of Shelbourne.

GIBSON, DON. The son-in-law of Sir Matt Busby, wing-half Don Gibson made 114 league and Cup appearances for Manchester United before joining Sheffield Wednesday in the summer of 1955. The following season he helped the Owls to win the second division championship but after being injured in the match at Swansea, he failed to get back in the side and had to be content with making just 27 appearances. He spent four years at Hillsborough but was plagued by injury problems throughout his stay and when he was fit, he faced severe competition from McAnearney and O'Donnell. Eventually losing his place to Tony Kay, he signed for Leyton Orient in June 1960, but because of the extent of his injuries, only played in eight league games before having to retire.

GLENNON, TED. Inside-forward Ted Glennon joined Wednesday from Grimsby Town in 1910 and after making his debut at Oldham Athletic, scored the winner against Spurs on his second appearance and both goals in the 2–1 victory over Bristol City on his third. He formed a very effective partnership up-front for Wednesday with David McLean, his unselfish approach making many a goal for the Scot. Glennon, too, scored his fair share of goals, 42 in 133 League and Cup appearances and another 54 in 117 wartime games, including four in a 5–0 win over Sheffield United at Bramall Lane on 16 March 1918. In fact, Glennon always seemed to score against the Blades and in 24 games scored 14 goals. When the war ended, Glennon took over as landlord of a local pub, but this was against club rules and he was allowed to leave and join Rotherham County.

GOALKEEPERS. Sheffield Wednesday FC has almost always been extremely well served by its goalkeepers and most of them have been very popular with the supporters – Jack Lyall, Teddy Davison, Jack Brown, Dave McIntosh, the Springett brothers and Martin Hodge. In the club's early days, they employed goalkeepers called Jim Smith and Bill Allan. Jim Smith, Wednesday's goalkeeper in the 1880s, was really called Jim Clarke, but he preferred to play under a pseudonym. When Bill Allan joined Wednesday in 1891, the club had no boots big enough to fit him. A cobbler in Sheffield worked through the night, making him a special pair. Scottish international goalkeeper Jack Lyall got his chance after the Frank Stubbs disaster of 1901 when the hapless keeper let in six goals in the match against Notts County. Stubbs had been kicked in the head and proceeded to let in six of the softest goals ever conceded in a league match. Lyall helped Wednesday win two league championships and the FA Cup in 1907. Teddy Davison at 5ft 7ins is in the record books as England's smallest goalkeeper. Adept at saving penalty kicks, sometimes two in a game, he played in 424 games for Wednesday before later managing Sheffield United. Jack Brown joined Wednesday from Worksop Town and after winning a second division championship medal in 1925–26, helped the Owls win two league championships and the FA Cup in 1935. The England international made 507 League and Cup appearances, the most by a Wednesday goalkeeper. Dave McIntosh was Wednesday's first-choice goalkeeper for the ten seasons after the Second World War. He won second division championship medals in 1951–52 and 1955–56 but a bad run of injuries, including breaking an arm twice inside a year, reduced his appearances to 308. Ron Springett has the distinction of being Wednesday's most-capped England player. An important member of the side that won the second division title in 1958–59, Springett played in 384 games for the Owls yet was never an ever-present. His brother Peter arrived at Hillsborough in the deal that took Ron to Loftus Road and made 207 appearances in eight seasons before losing his place to Peter Fox. Peter Fox was 15 years and 269 days old when he played for Wednesday at Orient in a division two game on 31 March 1973 – the club's youngest-ever player. Martin Hodge was one of the most consistent goalkeepers in the club's history. He played in 173 consecutive league games for the club and was Wednesday's keeper when Coventry's Steve Ogrizovic scored an astonishing goal. His clearance from the Leppings Lane End bounced once and with the aid of the wind, sailed over the Wednesday goalkeeper's head.

GOALS. The most goals Sheffield Wednesday have ever scored in one game was in their 12–0 victory over Halliwell in the first round of the FA Cup at Olive Grove on 17 January 1891. Woolhouse scored five, Cawley and R. Brandon two apiece and H. Brandon, Ingram and Mumford one each. In the League, Wednesday beat Birmingham City 9–1 in 1930–31 and Sunderland 8–0 in 1911–12.

GOALSCORING RECORDS. Jimmy Trotter's 37 goals in 1925–26 helped Wednesday win the second division championship and the following season, he again scored 37 goals, feats which remained club records until the emergence of Derek Dooley. In 1951–52, he scored 46 goals in just 30 league appearances, including five against Notts County and four in matches against Everton and Hull City. John Fantham, who scored 167 goals for Wednesday holds the club's post-war aggregate scoring record.

GOALS – CAREER BEST. The highest goalscorer in the club's history is Andrew Wilson who between season 1900–01 and the end of season 1914–15 had netted 216 goals for the club. These comprised 199 league goals and 17 FA Cup goals.

GOALS – INDIVIDUAL. The most goals scored by a Sheffield Wednesday player in any one match is six by Douglas Hunt in the 7–0 win over Norwich City at Hillsborough on 19 November 1938. A number of players have scored five goals in a game for Wednesday. Bob Gregory scored five on 1 November 1882 in the club's pre-league days when Wednesday beat Spilsby 12–2 in the first round of the FA Cup. Woolhouse also netted five when Halliwell were beaten 12–0 in the FA Cup first round of the 1890–91 season. The feat has been achieved three times in the Football League, twice by Jimmy Trotter. He hit all five goals in the home victory over Portsmouth on 13 December 1924 and five more nine months later when Stockport County were defeated 6–2. The last Wednesday player to score five goals in a league match was Derek Dooley as the Owls beat Notts County 6–0 on 3 November 1951.

GOALS – SEASON. The club's highest league goalscorer in any one season remains Derek Dooley who scored 46 league goals as Wednesday finished top of the second division in 1951–52. He also scored when Wednesday lost 2–1 in the FA Cup at Bradford. He scored five in Wednesday's 6–0 victory over Notts County, all four in the 4–0 win over Everton and four in the Owls' 6–0 win over Yorkshire rivals Hull City. He also scored two hat-tricks: West Ham United away 6–0 and Brentford away 3–2. It was an even more remarkable achievement because he missed the first 11 games of the season.

GRANT, DAVID. After joining Wednesday as an apprentice in July 1976, David Grant had to wait until Boxing Day 1977 before making his League debut at Tranmere Rovers, though he had played in the FA Cup defeat at Wigan Athletic nine days earlier. Under new manager Jack Charlton, Grant proved himself to be a very capable full-back, strong in the tackle and a good distributor of the ball. When Wednesday won promotion from the third division in 1979–80, he missed only three games and was a regular member of the Owls side in their first season back in the second division. In 1981–82, he lost his place to Charlie Williamson and moved to Oxford United. He played in 24 league games for the Manor Ground club, later going on loan to Chesterfield. He also played for Cardiff City, ending his career with Rochdale.

GREAT ESCAPE. On the morning of Good Friday 1928, Sheffield Wednesday were bottom of division one with 25 points from 34 matches and with little prospect of escaping relegation, as they were four points below Manchester United, their closest rivals. They began the long haul, captained by ex-Spurs player, Jimmy Seed, by beating Tottenham Hotspur 3–1 at White Hart Lane. Spurs were tenth with 35 points from 36 games before the match. Wednesday went on to win four and draw the other four of their remaining fixtures to avoid the drop. Middlesbrough and Tottenham Hotspur were the two teams to be relegated.

GRUMMITT, PETER. Making his League debut for Nottingham Forest against Bolton Wanderers on 12 November 1960, his first touch of the ball was to pick it out of his net after Jim Iley had put through his own goal in the opening minutes. Going on to make the number one shirt his own, he made 352 first-team appearances for Forest in nine seasons at the City Ground. He was an ever-present in 1966–67 when Forest reached the FA Cup semi-final and were runners-up in the first division. Capped three times by England at Under-23 level, he was surprisingly allowed to leave and in January 1970 he signed for Wednesday. Though he was unable to prevent the Owls being relegated in 1969–70, he missed just one game the following season before facing stiff competition from Peter Springett. He went on to play in 130 games for the club before he signed for Brighton after a short spell on loan. He played in 136 league games for the Seagulls before leaving the game.

GUEST PLAYERS. The guest system was used by all clubs during the two wars. Although on occasions it was abused almost beyond belief (some sides that opposed Wednesday had ten or even 11 guests) it normally worked quite sensibly and effectively to the benefit of players, clubs and supporters alike. Of the players who guested for the Owls, England international Ronnie Starling had already appeared in 193 games for the club, whilst Joe Cockcroft, who appeared in a record 217 consecutive league and Cup games for West Ham United, signed for Wednesday at the end of the war.

H

HARKES, JOHN. Signed for just £70,000, John Harkes had been spotted by Wednesday playing for the University of North Carolina and the USA national side. Despite being a natural midfielder, he replaced the injured Roland Nilsson at right-back and made his debut at home to Oldham Athletic in November 1990. By the end of his first season, he had helped the Owls to promotion from the second division and won a League Cup winners' medal after Wednesday had beaten Manchester United 1–0. Over the next few seasons he played in several different positions for the club and in 1992–93 he became the first American to score at Wembley when he shot past David Seaman after just nine minutes of the League Cup final. He had played in 118 first-team games for the Owls when in August 1993 he joined Derby County for £500,000. A popular player at the Baseball Ground, as he had been at Hillsborough, the USA Soccer Federation paid around £500,000 for his services in October 1995 and then loaned him back to West Ham United. He made his debut for the Hammers in a 1–0 win for the London club at Hillsborough. Now back in the States, he is captaining the national side.

HARPER, TED. A prolific goalscorer throughout his career, Ted Harper played with Whitstable and Sheppey before joining

Blackburn Rovers, the only league club prepared to take a chance on him. In his second season, 1924–25, he was the League's top scorer and the following season he finished with 43 goals from 37 games and won an England cap. He was transferred to Sheffield Wednesday in November 1927 and scored a hat-trick on his debut in a 6–4 win at Derby County. At Hillsborough, he suffered from injuries but when fully fit, couldn't win his place back in the side due to the form of Jack Allen. He had scored 16 goals in 22 appearances, yet was allowed to join Tottenham Hotspur. At White Hart Lane, he scored 83 goals in 78 matches. His record could have been even better but because of his reputation as a goalscorer, he often received some rough treatment from opponents and missed a number of matches through injury. In 1930–31, he scored 36 goals in only 30 league appearances to set a new Spurs record. Allowed to move to Preston North End, he showed he was still as sharp as ever by scoring 43 goals in 1932–33. This meant that he had the enviable record of having scored most goals in a season for three different clubs. At the start of the following season, his goals began to dry up and he was transferred back to Blackburn Rovers, his first league club.

HART, PAUL. The son of the former Manchester City forward and manager, Johnny Hart, Paul began his league career with Stockport County, making 88 appearances for the Edgeley Park club. Joining Blackpool in June 1973, Hart soon established himself with the Seasiders and in 1976–77, an ever-present, he scored six goals, as the club challenged for promotion. His reputation grew at Bloomfield Road and with Blackpool's relegation to division three virtually assured, he joined Leeds United for £300,000. He made over 200 appearances for the Elland Road club before moving to Nottingham Forest in the 1983 close season. Two years later, he joined Sheffield Wednesday on a free transfer. He soon proved his ability, adding authority to the Wednesday back four as they finished fifth in the first division in 1985–86. In December 1986, he was surprisingly transferred to Birmingham City and on his debut broke a leg. It proved to be his only game for the St Andrews club and in the summer of 1987 he joined Notts County as player–coach. He later managed Chesterfield to a Wembley play-off final.

HAT-TRICK HEROES. Alec Brady scored Wednesday's first league hat-trick on 14 October 1893 when the Sheffield club beat Derby County 4–0. Fred Spiksley scored the first hat-trick at Owlerton when Wednesday beat Luton Town 6–0 in December 1899 and marked his last appearance in representative football with a hat-trick for the Football League against the Scottish League. In June 1908, Frank Bradshaw made his England debut and scored a hat-trick in their 11–1 win over Austria in Vienna. Unbelievably, he never represented his country again. Ted Harper scored a hat-trick on his league debut for Wednesday in a 6–4 win at Derby County in November 1927. Douglas Hunt is the only player in the club's history to score a double hat-trick in a league match. He achieved this feat in Wednesday's 7–0 win over Norwich City on 19 November 1938. In the following match, a 5–1 defeat of Luton Town at Kenilworth Road he hit another hat-trick. Andy Blair scored a unique hat-trick of penalties in Wednesday's 4–2 League Cup win, also against Luton Town, at Hillsborough on 20 November 1984. Bolton referee, Tom Fitzharris awarded the spot-kicks in the 15th, 51st and 70th minutes.

HEMMINGFIELD, BILL. Bill Hemmingfield arrived at Wednesday after a spell with Mexborough Town, where he had earned a reputation as a goalscoring forward. In his first season at Olive Grove, he was the club's top scorer, with eight of the 24 scored as Wednesday suffered relegation for the first time in their history. At the end of that season, he was transferred to Grimsby Town but in 1903 he returned to Wednesday. In his second spell at the club, his appearances were mainly confined to the reserves and any first-team games he did play were at half-back or inside-forward.

HENDERSON, WILLIE. Joining Wednesday in the summer of 1972, the former Glasgow Rangers winger arrived with a reputation as something of a rebel. He had won every Scottish domestic honour with the Ibrox club before he had turned 19 and after winning his first cap against Wales in 1962 went on to appear in 29 full internationals for Scotland. Though his stay at Hillsborough was only short, the 29-year-old Henderson played with all the enthusiasm of a much younger player, helping to inspire the up-and-coming Eric Potts. His skills were still evident for all to see and it seemed surprising that manager Dooley had secured his services on a free transfer. Henderson played in 56 games in his two seasons with the club and though he scored only five goals, they were all memorable. He left Hillsborough in May 1974 to join Hong Kong Rangers.

HICKTON, JOHN. Chesterfield-born John Hickton joined Wednesday straight from school and made his debut at left-back in the match against Aston Villa in March 1964. He switched to centre-forward and, netting with great regularity in the Central League, was given his chance in the League side at home to Fulham in November 1964. He scored the Owls' goal in a 1–1 draw and played in the remaining 26 games of the season, scoring ten goals. The following season, he scored 11 goals in 25 games, including a hat-trick in a 4–0 win over Arsenal before rather surprisingly being allowed to join Middlesbrough in September 1966 for £20,000. At Ayresome Park, Hickton scored 159 goals in 415 league matches before ending his career with Hull City.

HILL, HAROLD. Signed from Notts County in October 1924, Harold Hill scored on his debut in a 2–0 win over Coventry City. In that 1924–25 season, Hill appeared in all five forward positions. The following season he settled into the inside-left position and played an important role in helping Wednesday win the second division title. He scored a number of memorable goals, including a superb hat-trick in a 4–1 win over Chelsea at Hillsborough. However, when Allen and Seed arrived at the club, Hill's first-team appearances were limited and in 1928 after scoring 40 goals in 99 games he moved to Scarborough, later ending his career with Chesterfield.

HILLSBOROUGH. Originally called Owlerton, it was seen as a major gamble when the club decided to move there in the summer of 1899. The area was very sparsely populated, four miles from the city centre and poorly served by public transport, though the area had been linked by a horse tramway since 1877. The land had belonged to James Willis Dixon, a wealthy silversmith, who, in 1892, had given over to Sheffield Corporation his home, Hillsborough Hall, for use as a library.

Described as meadowlands 'out in the wilds', Wednesday had to find £10,000 to purchase and prepare the ten-acre site. To do this, they hurriedly formed a limited company and only finalised the deal in April, four months before the start of the new season. The former stand at Olive Grove was re-erected on the north side at Owlerton to seat an extra 3,000 spectators and £200 was spent on a low cover for the Leppings Lane End. The first match at Owlerton was the second division fixture against Chesterfield on 2 September 1899 which Wednesday won 5–1. The ground wasn't isolated for long. By 1901, the city's new electric trams were serving the ground and in 1912 the club were asked, at short notice, to accommodate the FA Cup semi-final replay between Blackburn Rovers and West Bromwich Albion. The first major developments inside the ground came the following year when work began on the erection of a new stand and on building up the Spion Kop at the Penistone Road End. On the south side of the ground, a new stand designed by Archibald Leitch and costing £18,000 was built. It provided seating for 5,600 plus terracing for 3,000 standing spectators. In 1914 the club changed the official name of the ground to Hillsborough and on 10 January the South Stand opened for the FA Cup tie against Notts County which the Owls won 3–2. Though the ground's capacity was now over 50,000, a few weeks later on 4 February, a crowd of 43,050 for the FA Cup fourth round replay against Wolves seemed to be tightly packed in. So much so, that a wall collapsed and fans fell onto the terracing below. Play was stopped and 75 fans, three of whom were critically injured, were carried to the dressing-rooms for treatment. The Wolves keeper was also a casualty as he fainted at the sight of what he thought was a corpse. However, the wall was repaired and soon after that 57,143 spectators watched Wednesday play Aston Villa in the FA Cup quarter-final – at the time, the biggest crowd ever seen at a football match in Sheffield. In April 1920, Hillsborough staged its first international match when England played Scotland. A crowd of 25,536 saw the home side come from behind to win 5–4. The ground staged a further two FA Cup semi-finals and was expanded further in 1927 when the Leppings Lane End was enlarged. The ground's biggest attendance came on 17 February 1934 when 72,841 saw Wednesday draw 2–2 with the eventual FA Cup winners, Manchester City in a fifth-round tie. During the Second World War, Wednesday made great efforts to stage representative games and were rewarded with B internationals, inter-league games and, after the war, FA Cup semi-finals. Hillsborough's floodlights were first switched on for the Derek Dooley testimonial game on 9 March 1955 when a crowd of 55,000 saw an International XI beat a Sheffield XI 5–1. Following promotion in 1958–59, the club launched a debenture scheme to try to finance the building of a North Stand to replace the old wooden one. The new 10,000 seater cantilever stand which cost £150,000 was formally opened by Sir Stanley Rous before the game with Bolton Wanderers on 23 August 1961. Just over a year later, Hillsborough was chosen as the venue for the European Nations International between England and France. In 1965 the terracing in front of the South Stand was converted to provide 3,300 uncovered seats. Also the stand and rooftop scoreboard at the Leppings Lane End were demolished and replaced by a new 4,465 seater West Stand at a cost of £110,000. By now, the ground was an obvious choice as a venue for the 1966 World Cup and staged four matches. A new club lounge was built and a sports hall erected behind the North Stand, used during the World Cup as a press centre. In 1986, £1 million was spent on building a roof over the exposed Kop and in adding terracing to both rear corners. Thus, Hillsborough became the only English football ground to grow since the Safety of Sports Grounds Act. The Kop roof was formally opened on 12 December 1986 by the Queen. In spite of being one of the safest grounds in the country, 95 Liverpool fans died at the Leppings Lane End on 15 April 1989 as Hillsborough staged the FA Cup semi-final between Liverpool and Nottingham Forest. Lord Justice Taylor's Interim Report made it clear that mistakes had been made, not only on the day, but in the previous ten years of safety management at the ground. Since that day, over £10 million has been spent on ground improvements, and following Hillsborough's selection as one of the venues for the 1996 European Championship, it remains one of England's top football grounds.

HIRST, DAVID. Following a meteoric rise with Barnsley, where he made his league debut in August 1985 three months prior to turning professional, David Hirst signed for Sheffield Wednesday

David Hirst

at the end of that season for £200,000. His first three seasons at Hillsborough were disappointing but in 1989–90 he began to make his mark, scoring 14 goals as Wednesday were relegated to the second division. In 1990–91 he scored 24 goals to help Wednesday win promotion at the first time of asking. He also won a League Cup winners' medal, following the Owls' 1–0 victory over Manchester United. At the end of that successful season, he was called up by England manager Graham Taylor for the tour of Australasia, where he made his international debut. In 1991–92, he scored three minutes into the new season against Aston Villa and continued in similar vein, ending the campaign with 21 league and Cup goals. Hirst scored his 100th goal for the club to take the 1993 FA Cup final to a replay but unfortunately he couldn't repeat the feat in the second game and had to settle for a losers' medal. Due to a number of injury-laden seasons, his 100th league goal for the club came in the 5–2 home defeat by Everton towards the end of the 1995–96 season in which David Pleat almost transferred him to the Goodison Park club. For all Owls' fans there is no finer sight than to see David Hirst bearing down on the opposition's goal.

HODGE, MARTIN. Southport-born goalkeeper Martin Hodge began his league career with Plymouth Argyle before joining Everton in the summer of 1979 for £135,000. He helped the Goodison Park club reach the semi-finals of the FA Cup the following season but was then injured and lost his place. Following loan spells with Preston North End (twice), Oldham Athletic and Gillingham, he signed for Sheffield Wednesday in August 1983 for £50,000. Making his Owls debut in a 1–0 win over Swansea City at Vetch Field on the opening day of the 1983–84 season, Hodge went on to be an ever-present in the next four seasons, playing in 173 consecutive league games immediately following his first-team debut. In 1986, he was made club captain and was put on stand-by for England's World Cup final squad in Mexico. He left Hillsborough in August 1988 to join Leicester City, playing in 75 league games for the Filbert Street club before moving to Hartlepool United.

HOLSGROVE, JOHN. After starting his league career with Crystal Palace, John Holsgrove moved to Wolverhampton

Martin Hodge

Wanderers in May 1965 for £18,000. It was at Molineux that Wolves' manager Bill McGarry converted the 6ft 2in wing-half into a central defender. He helped the club to win promotion to the first division and in three seasons in the top flight only missed a handful of games. He was then injured and in June 1971, after playing in 180 league games for Wolves, signed for Wednesday for £50,000. Taking over the captaincy, he played in 115 first-team games for the Owls before being given a free transfer in the summer of 1975 after the club had been relegated to the third division. He joined Stockport County but after the Edgeley Park side had finished the 1975–76 season near the bottom of the fourth division, he hung up his boots.

HOME MATCHES. Wednesday's best home wins are the 12–0 rout of Halliwell in the first-round FA Cup match on 17 January 1891 and the 12–2 win against Spilsby on 4 November 1882 in the club's pre-league days. In the League, Wednesday beat Birmingham City 9–1 on 13 December 1930, whilst the club's worst home defeat is 7–1, a scoreline inflicted upon them by Nottingham Forest in 1994–95. Wednesday have scored eight goals in a home match on two occasions – against Sunderland in division one, 1911–12, and against Spora Luxembourg in the UEFA Cup first round first leg, 1992–93 – both times winning 8–0.

HOME SEASONS. Sheffield Wednesday have gone through a complete league season with an undefeated home record on four occasions: 1899–1900, 1903–04, 1928–29 and 1934–35. In 1899–1900, the Owls won all 17 of their home matches in winning the second division championship whilst the club's highest number of home wins in a league season is 18. This was achieved in 1928–29 from 21 matches, as the club won the first division title.

HONOURS. The major honours achieved by the club are:

First Division Championship	1902–03, 1903–04, 1928–29, 1929–30
Second Division Championship	1899–1900, 1925–26, 1951–52, 1955–56, 1958–59
FA Cup Winners	1896, 1907, 1935
League Cup Winners	1991
FA Charity Shield	1935

HOOPER, MARK. Wednesday manager Bob Brown once told the 5ft 5½in winger who wore size 4 boots that he was too small to make the grade in league football. Yet Hooper helped his home-town club Darlington win the third division (north) championship in 1924–25 and the following season produced a masterly performance as the Quakers beat Wednesday 5–1, despite the Owls winning the second division title. Brown altered his opinion of Hooper and in January 1927, persuaded him to sign for Wednesday for £2,000. One of the best uncapped wingers of his day, Hooper was a model of consistency and between 6 April 1928 and 23 April 1932 played in 189 consecutive league and Cup games. In 1927–28, Hooper scored some vital goals as the Owls were unbeaten over the last ten games of the season to avoid relegation, including a hat-trick in a 4–2 win over Tottenham Hotspur. An ever-present in Wednesday's league championship winning seasons of 1928–29 and 1929–30, he also won an FA Cup winners' medal in 1935, scoring one of the goals in a 4–2 win over

West Bromwich Albion. Of all his goals, he is probably best remembered for his brilliant equaliser against Arsenal in the sixth round of the Cup-winning season. Hooper and England international Ellis Rimmer were the best pair of wingers in club football at that time. The little man was never outshone and scored 136 goals in 423 appearances before leaving Hillsborough to join Rotherham United as coach.

HORNSBY, BRIAN. A former England schoolboy and youth international, Brian Hornsby began his league career with Arsenal, playing in 33 games before joining Shrewsbury Town from where he became Jack Charlton's first major signing as Wednesday manager. He made his debut at Lincoln City in March 1978, replacing the unfortunate Paul Bradshaw who had to leave the game through injury. He scored three goals in Wednesday's epic FA Cup struggle against Arsenal in 1978–79 and the following season played a key role in the club's promotion from the third division. He lost his place midway through the 1980–81 season and had a loan spell at Chester before playing in North America with Edmonton Drillers. He ended his league career with Carlisle United, for whom he made nine league appearances, playing one game on loan with Chesterfield during his time at Brunton Park.

HUDSON, JACK. A strong-tackling defender in Wednesday's early years, Jack Hudson helped the club win a number of local Cup finals and was in the side that reached the FA Cup semi-final for the first time in 1882. He won a number of representative honours, making 24 appearances for the Sheffield FA and playing twice for the North against the South before making his international debut for England in the 7–0 win over Ireland at Liverpool in 1883. Hudson was a member of the group that tried to persuade the club to adopt professionalism and after undertaking secretarial duties following Bob Littlehales' illness, he became club captain in 1887. Not long after, he suffered a serious injury which meant that his playing days were restricted and he began to concentrate on coaching. In 1889, a few months after his benefit match, he joined the newly formed Sheffield United.

HUMPHREYS, RITCHIE. The young stocky striker broke

through into the Wednesday first team towards the end of the 1995–96 season but it was at the beginning of the 1996–97 campaign that he made a name for himself. Scoring on his home debut against Aston Villa on the opening day of the season, he scored three goals in the first four games, which were all won by Wednesday. A level-headed and versatile player, Ritchie Humphreys should play an important role in the future of Sheffield Wednesday.

HUNDRED GOALS. Sheffield Wednesday have scored more than 100 league goals in a season on five occasions. The highest total is 106 goals, scored in 1958–59 when they won the second division championship. The Owls scored 105 goals in winning the first division championship of 1929–30 and 102 the following season when they finished third. They scored exactly 100 goals in 1951–52 when winning the second division championship and 101 in 1955–56 when the Owls again won the division two title following relegation the previous season. The club have only ever conceded 100 goals in a season on one occasion and that was in 1954–55 when they finished bottom of the first division.

HUNT, DOUGLAS. The Salisbury-born forward began his footballing career with Winchester City before being introduced to league football with Tottenham Hotspur in 1934. After a couple of years at White Hart Lane, he joined Barnsley and it was from there that he transferred to Wednesday in March 1938 for £3,000. When he arrived at Hillsborough, the Owls were near the foot of the second division and relegation seemed a distinct possibility. Hunt's goals helped them avoid the drop and in 1938–39 he became a major figure in the club's bid for promotion to the first division. On 19 November 1938, he became the only player in the club's history to score six goals in a league match when Norwich City were beaten 7–0 at Hillsborough. A week later, he hit a hat-trick as the Owls beat Luton Town 5–1 at Kenilworth Road. He ended the season as the club's top scorer with 24 goals in 30 League appearances but Wednesday failed by one point to clinch a promotion place. Though he played a few games for Wednesday during the war, most of his football was played with Brentford. When league football was resumed in 1946, he joined Leyton Orient.

HUNT, GEORGE. Known as the 'Chesterfield Tough', George Hunt was turned down by Sheffield United, despite scoring four goals in a trial game. After starting his league career with the Saltergate club, he joined Tottenham Hotspur in June 1930. Deputising for Ted Harper, Hunt netted five goals in eight games but Spurs lost six of those games and missed out on promotion. However, the Spurs management persevered with Hunt and in 1932–33 his 33 goals helped the club back into division one. Around this time he won three England caps but after Jack Tresadern's appointment as Spurs manager, he played less of a part in the team and in October 1937 he joined Arsenal. He spent six months at Highbury before moving to Bolton Wanderers. A regular for the Trotters during the war, he helped them win the League Cup (North) in 1945. He signed for Sheffield Wednesday in November 1946 but after scoring nine goals in 35 games, he was allowed to rejoin Bolton, where he served on the training staff for over 20 years.

HUNTER, JACK. Hunter began his career with Heeley and arrived at Wednesday from Sheffield Albion in 1880, after a spell with Providence. He played in the club's first FA Cup tie on 18 December 1880 when they beat Blackburn Rovers 4–0 but he didn't stay with the club for long. One of the first players from the Sheffield area to exploit professionalism before it had been legalised, he joined Blackburn Olympic in 1882. When they won the FA Cup the following year, Hunter was the star of their 2–1 extra-time win over Old Etonians. Between 1878 and 1882, Hunter played in seven internationals for England, captaining his country in the 1–0 defeat by Wales at Blackburn in 1881. He later joined Blackburn Rovers and played against Wednesday in the very first match held at Olive Grove. When his playing days were over, he stayed with Rovers as trainer and groundsman.

HYDE, GRAHAM. A terrier-like midfield player, Graham Hyde made his debut for the Owls against Manchester City in September 1991 in place of the injured John Sheridan. A vital first-team fringe player, he makes up for his lack of inches with his wholehearted displays, showing vision and excellent passing ability. Though he has appeared in over 160 first-team games for Wednesday, he has been surprisingly left out of the side on certain occasions and is viewed as a substitute rather than a starter. Doncaster-born Hyde has a good footballing brain and with his insatiable workrate should be a regular first-teamer for years to come.

I

INJURIES. The risk of serious injury is a constant threat in the game of football and all professional players expect to miss games through injury at some point in their careers. However, on 14 February 1953, Derek Dooley, Wednesday's goalscoring sensation, was carried off in the 59th minute of the match against Preston North End at Deepdale after colliding with George Thompson, North End's keeper. While he lay in hospital, complications set in and in order to save his life, surgeons had to amputate the limb.

INTER CITIES FAIRS CUP. Wednesday's first match in the Inter Cities Fairs Cup in September 1961 saw them go down 4–2 at Olympique Lyonnais but in the second leg at Hillsborough three weeks later, the Owls won 5–2 to give them a 7–6 aggregate win. Facing AS Roma in the second round, Wednesday continued to produce good home form, beating the Italians 4–0 with makeshift centre-forward Gerry Young netting a hat-trick. Despite losing 1–0 in Italy, the Owls progressed to the quarter-finals where they faced Barcelona. Two goals from John Fantham and one from Alan Finney helped Wednesday win the home leg 3–2 but despite a fine rearguard defence in the Nou Camp Stadium, the Spanish side won 2–0 to go through 4–3 on aggregate. The club's next Inter Cities Fairs Cup campaign was in 1963–64 when they beat DOS Utrecht 4–1 both home and away to win 8–2 on aggregate.

'Bronco' Layne scored a hat-trick in the Hillsborough leg. In round two, Wednesday lost 3–2 at FC Koln but despite applying constant pressure in the home tie, the visitors won 2–1 to end Wednesday's interest in the competition.

INTERNATIONAL MATCHES. Hillsborough has staged a number of international matches. The first was on 10 April 1920 when England came from behind to beat Scotland 5–4. In 1962, Hillsborough hosted the European Nations international between England and France. Wednesday's Ron Springett was in goal in a game that ended 1–1. During the 1966 World Cup finals, Hillsborough hosted three group games involving West Germany, Spain, Switzerland and Argentina and a quarter-final tie between West Germany and Uruguay. In 1973, Northern Ireland played Bulgaria at Hillsborough but only 6,292 turned up to see the two sides play out a goalless draw. In 1996, Hillsborough staged three European Championship games involving Denmark, Turkey, Croatia and Portugal.

INTERNATIONAL PLAYERS. Sheffield Wednesday's most-capped player (i.e. caps gained while players were registered with the club) is Nigel Worthington with 50 caps. The following is a complete list of players who have gained full international honours for England, Scotland, Wales, Northern Ireland and the Republic of Ireland:

England		J. Stewart	2
B. Betts	1	A. Strange	20
E. Blenkinsop	26	P. Swan	19
F. Bradshaw	1	D. Walker	1
T. Brayshaw	1	G. Wilson	12
T. Brittleton	5	C. Woods	19
J. Brown	6	G. Young	1
H. Burgess	4	*Scotland*	
H. Burrows	3	J. Blair	2
T. Catlin	5	J. Campbell	1
C. Clegg	1	J. Lyall	1
W. Clegg	2	J. McCalliog	4
T. Crawshaw	10	D. McLean	1
H. Davis	3	G. Robertson	3
T. Davison	1	A. Wilson	6

J. Fantham	1	*Wales*	
B. Felton	1	H. Hanford	4
R. Froggatt	4	R. Jones	1
D. Hirst	3	T. Jones	1
J. Hudson	1	M. Pembridge	18
F. Kean	7	P. Rodrigues	16
T. Leach	2	R. Williams	4
B. Marsden	3	D. Witcomb	1
W. Mosforth	9	*Northern Ireland*	
C. Palmer	18	D. Clements	13
A. Quixall	5	R. Coyle	5
E. Rimmer	4	W. Gowdy	1
J. Robinson	4	E. McConnell	5
H. Ruddlesdin	3	J. Murray	1
J. Sewell	6	P. O'Connell	2
A. Sinton	2	S. Todd	3
F. Spiksley	7	N. Worthington	50
R. Springett	33	*Republic of Ireland*	
R. Starling	1	B. Fallon	2
G. Stephenson	1	E. Gannon	11
M. Sterland	1	J. Sheridan	27

The first Sheffield Wednesday player to be capped was Charles Clegg who played for England v Scotland in 1872.

ISLE OF MAN. On 17 May 1948, Sheffield Wednesday played Sheffield United in Douglas, Isle of Man in a friendly. It was the first game between professionals ever staged on the island. The result was a 2–2 draw, in front of 8,000 spectators.

J

JEMSON, NIGEL. After displaying a precocious talent with his local club, Preston North End, Nigel Jemson was signed by Nottingham Forest in March 1988 for £150,000 but before he played a game for the City Ground club, he was loaned out to Bolton Wanderers and back to North End to gain more experience. He had been at the City Ground for almost two years before he made his debut, ending that season by scoring the only goal of the 1990 League Cup final. He made a good start to the following season, but despite scoring a hat-trick in a fifth-round FA Cup win over Southampton, he was not selected for the Cup final against Tottenham Hotspur. He joined Sheffield Wednesday in September 1991 for a fee of £800,000 but struggled to make much of an impact in his early games, with the exception of the Owls' 3–2 win over Manchester United, when he came on for Hirst and scored two late goals. He played in 51 league games for Wednesday with almost half his appearances coming as substitute. After a loan spell at Grimsby Town, he joined Notts County early in the 1994–95 season. More loan spells followed, with Watford and Rotherham United before he signed for Oxford United in July 1996.

JOHNSON, JEFF. A former Welsh schoolboy, youth and Under-23 international, Jeff Johnson played for Manchester City and

Nigel Jemson

Swansea before joining Malcolm Allison at Crystal Palace. He had played in 87 league games for the Eagles when Allison gave the Cardiff-born midfielder a free transfer. Wednesday snapped him up and he made his debut in the opening game of the 1976–77 season, a goalless draw at home to Walsall. When the Owls won promotion to the second division in 1979–80, Johnson was voted the supporters' Player of the Year. He had appeared in 211 first-team games when Len Ashurst, who was then manager of Newport County, took him to Somerton Park for £60,000. He made 34 league appearances for the Welsh side, before later playing for Gillingham and Port Vale.

JOHNSON, PETER. Joining Wednesday in December 1957 from Rotherham United, Peter Johnson made his debut in a 4–4 draw at home to Preston North End. Most of his 207 first-team games for the Owls were played at full-back, though he occasionally turned out as an emergency centre-forward. He was an ever-present in 1960–61 when Wednesday were runners-up in the first division but after playing his last game in the 3–2 win over

Sheffield United on 2 January 1965, he was allowed to join Peterborough United.

JOICEY, BRIAN. Winlanton-born Brian Joicey played his early football with North Shields and in 1968–69, he scored 45 goals for the club, including the winning goal in the FA Amateur Cup final at Wembley. He also represented an FA XI against the UAU at Hillsborough, scoring four goals. It was this sort of form that persuaded Bob Dennison to take him to Coventry City in June 1969. At Highfield Road he scored ten goals in 31 league games before arriving at Hillsborough in August 1971 along with Dave Clements. It didn't take him long to make his mark; in his first season, he scored all three goals in a 3–1 home win over Orient. The following season, he bagged another hat-trick as Wednesday beat Crystal Palace 3–2 at Villa Park in a fourth-round FA Cup replay. He continued to score with regularity in 1973–74 but in the following campaign he was hampered by injuries and lost his place. After scoring 53 goals in 164 first-team appearances, the popular Geordie joined Barnsley. He scored 43 goals in 93 league appearances for the Oakwell club, before ill health forced him to retire.

JONES, RYAN. Welsh international Ryan Jones is a local discovery who became a regular member of the first-team squad towards the end of the 1992–93 season after making his debut against Coventry City on 3 March 1993. Hampered by injuries, the left-sided midfielder was loaned out to Scunthorpe United during the 1995–96 season and after scoring three goals in 11 appearances for the Irons is now back at Hillsborough hoping to stake another claim for first-team football.

JORDAN, CLARRIE. Starting his league career with Doncaster Rovers, Clarrie Jordan scored 44 goals in 1946–47 to help the Belle Vue club win the third division (north) title with a record 72 points. He signed for Wednesday in February 1948 for a fee of £6,000 with Sheffield inside-forward Arthur Lowes going in the opposite direction. Jordan scored on his debut in a 3–1 win over Bradford but was never the prolific scorer he had been with Rovers. He did, however, score four goals when Wednesday beat Hull City 6–2 in September 1949, ending the season with 12 goals in 26 games to finish second in the club's goalscoring charts. He suffered a number of injuries during his career, the worst a badly swollen knee which later developed arthritis. He was forced to retire in 1955 at the age of 33 and some 30 years later had to have both of his legs amputated.

K

KAY, TONY. Though he made his first-team debut in 1954, red-haired Tony Kay didn't become a first-team regular until the arrival of manager Harry Catterick four years later. He played in seven England Under-23 matches and represented the Football League on three occasions. An ever-present in seasons 1960–61 and 1961–62, Kay went on to play in 203 league and Cup games before being transferred to Everton in December 1962 for £55,000 (then a record fee for a half-back). In 1963 he won his one and only England cap when he scored in the 8–1 win over Switzerland in Zurich. Appointed captain during Harry Catterick's reign as Everton manager, he played a leading role in the championship success of 1962–63. However, he was at the centre of football's greatest-ever scandal when in 1965, he was sent to prison and banned for life after the infamous soccer bribes trial. It was a very sad end to the career of a man who was without doubt one of the most talented wing-halves of his day.

KEAN, FRED. Though he was born in Sheffield, Fred Kean began his career as an inside-forward for Portsmouth. After he moved to Wednesday in June 1920, he played most of his games at wing-half or centre-half. When Wednesday won the second division championship in 1925–26, Kean was an England international, having won his first cap against Belgium in 1923. He gained seven of his nine caps while with the Owls. In 1926–27, he succeeded

91

Frank Froggatt as Wednesday captain but towards the end of the following season, he lost his place in the club's 'Great Escape' to Tony Leach and the captaincy to Jimmy Seed. He left Hillsborough in September 1928, to join Bolton Wanderers, thus missing out on the club's league championship successes. However, at Burnden Park, he helped the Trotters win the FA Cup in 1929 and made 89 appearances before leaving to end his career with Luton Town.

KENNY, VIN. A strong-tackling full-back who could play on either flank, Vin Kenny made his league debut for Wednesday in a 5–3 win at Leicester City in September 1946. In 1949–50, he played in all but two of Wednesday's league games (both defeats) as the Owls gained promotion from the second division. After relegation the following season, Jones played left-back in 1951–52 as Wednesday won the second division championship. Never a player to shirk a challenge, he was dismissed during Wednesday's 3–1 third-round FA Cup replay win over Sheffield United at Bramall Lane in 1954 following a more than enthusiastic tackle on Jimmy Hagan. He played in 152 first-team games for Wednesday before moving to Carlisle United and playing in 103 league games for the Brunton Park club.

KILSHAW, EDDIE. After beginning his footballing career with Bury in 1937, wartime service with the RAF hampered his progress, though once he returned to Gigg Lane after the hostilities, it didn't take him long to make an impression. Wednesday were one of a number of clubs to show interest in the talented player and signed him in December 1948 for £20,000, a record fee for a winger. Unfortunately, Kilshaw was to make only 19 appearances in a Wednesday shirt, for in the game against Leicester City at Hillsborough on 11 April 1949, he suffered a dislocated knee and was forced to quit the game. Even during that short period, Kilshaw had displayed enough of his talent to indicate that he would have been a great favourite with the Owls' fans.

KING, PHIL. An attacking left-back, Bristol-born Phil King played his early football with Exeter City and Torquay United before joining Swindon Town in February 1987. He helped the Robins win promotion to the second division and was an ever-present in 1987–88. It came as no surprise when Wednesday, who were then in the first division, signed him in November 1989. Unfortunately, the Owls were relegated at the end of his first season at Hillsborough but he missed only three league games in 1990–91 as the club won promotion at the first attempt. He also picked up a League Cup winners' medal and missed only four games the following season when Wednesday finished third in the top flight. In August 1992, he suffered a cruciate ligament injury which kept him out of the team for months. Once fully fit, he found it difficult to win his place back on a regular basis and after a loan spell at Notts County, joined Aston Villa for £250,000 in August 1994. With Alan Wright and Steve Staunton also fighting for the left-back spot, King was loaned out to West Bromwich Albion but suffered a second cruciate ligament injury in November 1995.

KIRKMAN, SAM. A fast, direct winger, Sam Kirkman was signed from Carlisle United in September 1909 as the club sought to find a replacement for Harry Davis. He scored on his debut at home to Bury but Wednesday went down 4–1. Though he created chances for others, he scored 39 goals in 202 appearances for Wednesday, including two in the 3–3 draw against Sheffield United at Bramall Lane, in his first season with the club. He also hit two goals in the 8–0 Boxing Day win over Sunderland in 1911 and in the 5–1 last day of the season win at West Bromwich Albion in 1912. He returned to Hillsborough after the First World War but played in only six games before joining Bury.

KNIGHTON, KEN. Knighton's early football experience was limited to Texborough, near Barnsley, but the youngster was saved from a career in mining by joining Wolverhampton Wanderers as an apprentice professional. Switching from inside-left to wing-half, he made 16 league appearances before moving to Oldham Athletic in November 1966. At Boundary Park, he caught the eye of a number of talent spotters and a year later joined Preston North End. His non-stop endeavour earned him popularity with the Deepdale fans, but in the summer of 1969, he was on the move again, this time to Blackburn Rovers. He made 70 league appearances for the Ewood Park club, scoring 11 goals before he joined his fifth league club, Hull City in March 1971. It was from Boothferry Park that Wednesday manager Derek Dooley signed him in August 1973. Within months of his arrival, Dooley had departed to be replaced by Steve Burtenshaw. The Owls were desperately trying to avoid relegation and it took a Knighton goal four minutes from the end of Wednesday's final match of the season against Bolton Wanderers to save them. However, even Knighton's determination and grit couldn't save them the following season and in January 1976 he retired to become youth-team coach. He later became coach at Roker Park before taking over as manager in June 1979. He took the club to runners-up spot in the second division, but was dismissed in April 1981, being considered inflexible. He later managed Orient before moving into non-league football.

L

LANGLEY, AMBROSE. Long-serving left-back Ambrose Langley played in 317 games for the Owls, helping them win the FA Cup in 1896. He was was an ever-present in the 1902–03 championship-winning side. Langley had played his early football with Boston and Grimsby Town but joined Wednesday from Middlesbrough Ironopolis. A great fighter, he suffered from knee injuries throughout his career and Aston Villa refused to sign him because the stubborn defender refused to undergo a medical. Wednesday decided to gamble and took him on trust. It was a wise decision, for Langley, who was one of the great favourites of the Wednesday fans, went on to give 11 seasons of sterling service. Occasionally his refusal to accept defeat led him into trouble with referees and in the famous FA Cup battle of 1900 against Sheffield United, he was sent off for ending Walter Bennett's interest in the game. A natural leader, he captained Wednesday to the second division title in 1900 and the league championship in 1902–03 and 1903–04. He was badly injured in the match at Sunderland in October 1903 and though he played in one more game, scoring Wednesday's goal from the penalty spot in a 1–1 draw with Newcastle United, he had to retire earlier than he would have wished. He later had a long career in management with Hull City and Huddersfield Town.

LARGEST CROWD. It was on 17 February 1934 that Hillsborough housed its largest crowd. The occasion was the FA Cup fifth-round match against Manchester City. A staggering crowd of 72,841 saw Wednesday draw 2–2 with goals from Rimmer and Dewar.

LAST MINUTE – NO GOAL. The referee's final whistle can never have been so important as at the end of the FA Cup semi-final game between Sheffield Wednesday and Huddersfield Town on 22 March 1930. As the final whistle was blown, a shot from Wednesday's Jack Allen was entering the net, but the referee refused to allow the goal because the ball had not crossed the line when the whistle was blown and Huddersfield won 2–1.

LATE FINISHES. Sheffield Wednesday's final match of the season against Chesterfield at Saltergate on 7 June 1947 is the latest date for the finish of any Owls' season.

LAYNE, DAVID. 'Bronco' Layne, as he was popularly known, began his career as a part-timer with Rotherham United in 1957, but two years later was given a free transfer and joined Swindon Town. After scoring 28 goals in 41 league appearances, he signed for Bradford City in December 1960 for a club record fee of £6,000. In 1961–62, Layne scored 34 league goals – a club record – and still the most goals scored by a City player in a single season. Having produced this remarkable strike rate, it was inevitable that sooner or later he would leave Valley Parade. In May 1962, he joined Sheffield Wednesday for a club record incoming fee of £22,500 (£20,000 plus the balance after Layne had played in ten division one games for the Hillsborough club). He continued his prolific goalscoring and in each of his two seasons with the Owls, finished as top scorer. In 1962–63, he scored 29 league goals, including a hat-trick in a 4–1 win over Manchester City, and in 1963–64, scored 23 goals in the League with another hat-trick in a 4–1 defeat of Ipswich Town at Portman Road. Layne was one of a number of people imprisoned and banned from the game for life for his part in the infamous bribes scandal. The ban was lifted in 1972 and Layne rejoined Wednesday. Unable to regain his place, he went on loan to Hereford United before playing non-league football with Matlock Town.

LAYTON, WILLIE. A miner at Blackwell Colliery, Willie Layton missed his nightshift in order to be in tip-top condition for his trial at Olive Grove and that very night, seven of his workmates lost their lives in an explosion. Signed by Wednesday in 1895, Layton had to wait until January 1898 before making his debut at Everton. Even then his only games in the Wednesday side were as a replacement for Langley or Earp. By 1899–1900, Layton had become an established member of the Sheffield side and won a second division championship medal. A strong-tackling full-back with a powerful kick, Layton appeared for the Football League against the Irish League in 1901 and won first division championship medals in 1902–03 and 1903–04.

LEACH, TONY. Signed from Wath Athletic in 1925–26, Tony Leach, who had failed a trial with Liverpool, soon settled into the Wednesday side after making his debut at home to Blackburn Rovers in February 1927. He started his footballing life as a forward before moving to wing-half, but the turning point in his career came when he was converted into a centre-half. Displacing Fred Kean in the heart of the Owls defence, he was an important member of the side which won the first division championship in seasons 1928–29 and 1929–30. His form over these two seasons led to him winning two caps for England in the winter of 1930 against Northern Ireland and Wales. Losing his place to Walter Millership towards the end of the 1933–34 season, he joined Newcastle United. He later moved to Stockport County, helping them to win the third division (north) championship, and ended his career with Carlisle United and Lincoln City.

LEADING GOALSCORERS. Sheffield Wednesday have provided the Football League's divisional leading goalscorer on six occasions:

1911–12	David McLean, Division One	25 goals
1912–13	David McLean, Division One	30
1926–27	Jimmy Trotter, Division One	37
1947–48	Eddie Quigley, Division Two	23
1951–52	Derek Dooley, Division Two	46
1979–80	Terry Curran, Division Three	22

LEAGUE GOALS – CAREER HIGHEST. Andrew Wilson holds the Hillsborough record for the most league goals with a career total of 199 goals between 1900 and 1920.

LEAGUE GOALS – LEAST CONCEDED. During the 1899–1900 season, Wednesday conceded just 22 goals in 34 games when winning the second division championship. The least goals Wednesday have conceded in a season of 42 games is 34 when the club won promotion to the first division in 1983–84.

LEAGUE GOALS – MOST INDIVIDUAL. Derek Dooley holds the Sheffield Wednesday record for the most league goals in a season with 46 scored in 1951–52 when the Owls won the second division championship.

LEAGUE GOALS – MOST SCORED. Wednesday's highest goal tally in the League was during the second division championship winning season of 1958–59 when they scored 106 goals.

LEAGUE NORTH WAR CUP FINAL. In 1942–43, Wednesday reached the League North War Cup final, a knock-out competition played over two legs. After beating Bradford City 2–1 on aggregate in the first round, Wednesday were beaten 1–0 at Nottingham Forest in the first leg of the second-round tie. The Owls won the home leg 5–1 with Frank Melling scoring four of the goals. A 3–2 win at Hillsborough, followed by a goalless draw at Bramall Lane, took Wednesday into the semi-finals at the expense of Sheffield United. In the semi-finals, York City were beaten 4–1 on aggregate to set up a two-legged final against Blackpool. After drawing the first leg at Bloomfield Road 2–2, the Owls went down 2–1 at home in front of a wartime record crowd of 47,657 to give the Seasiders the trophy 4–3 on aggregate.

LEAGUE VICTORY – HIGHEST. Wednesday's best league victory is the 9–1 win over Birmingham City at Hillsborough on 13 December 1930. Mark Hooper hit a hat-trick, Jack Ball and Jimmy Seed scored two goals apiece with one each from Harry Burgess and Ellis Rimmer. Wednesday also beat Sunderland 8–0 on Boxing Day 1911 with David McLean scoring four of the goals.

LITTLEWOODS CUP. See Football League Cup

LLOYD, BILLY. One of the club's earliest utility players, Billy Lloyd joined Wednesday from Jarrow in the summer of 1906 and though he only appeared in six league games in his first season, he was selected as reserve for the FA Cup final against Everton. His best position was at outside-right but after Sam Kirkman's arrival in 1909, he switched to wing-half, even playing at inside-forward and centre-half. A loyal clubman, he had appeared in 85 games for Wednesday when he was given a free transfer in 1913 and joined Rotherham County. After the First World War, he returned to Hillsborough as a member of the groundstaff.

LOFTHOUSE, JIMMY. A diminutive outside-left, Jimmy Lofthouse began his career with Stalybridge Celtic before joining Reading, from where he was signed by Wednesday in August 1920. Wednesday had just been relegated from the first division and he was one of manager Bob Brown's first signings as he tried to revive the Owls' flagging fortunes. Lofthouse's first three games were all goalless draws, but he played his part in trying to lift the gloom that descended on Hillsborough. A steady rather than spectacular winger, he played in a run of 76 consecutive league games, which ended in December 1922 following the arrival of Horace Henshall from Notts County. The St Helens-born player moved to Rotherham United, later playing with Bristol Rovers.

LONG SERVICE. For the entire pre-First World War period, Sheffield Wednesday resisted the temptation to appoint a manager, preferring to leave their affairs in the capable hands of Arthur Dickinson, working in conjunction with the board. It was a policy that served the club well. Dickinson was first connected with the club in 1887 and became honorary secretary from 1891 to 1920. He led the Owls to the first division title twice, the second division once and to two FA Cup finals. When Wednesday finished bottom of the first division in 1919–20, the club's attitude changed and Bob Brown was appointed the 'first professional secretary–manager'. He lasted for 13 years in the job and restored the club's playing fortunes. Only Eric Taylor stayed longer. Taylor joined Wednesday as an office boy in 1929 and finished as general manager in 1974, managing the club between 1942 and 1958. Another long-serving member of the Wednesday club was Eric England who spent 47 years with the Owls. Starting as an office junior in 1936, he was general secretary when he retired in 1983. On the playing side, a number of players have given long service to the Owls. They include Tom Brittleton (1905–1920), Jack Brown (1923–1937), Teddy Davison (1908–1925), Alan Finney (1951–1966), Redfern Froggatt (1943–1960) and Andrew Wilson (1900–1920).

LOWDELL, ARTHUR. Always known as 'Darkie', Arthur Lowdell arrived from Ton Pentrie in January 1922 as an inside-right. In a later spell at outside-right, he kept Rees Williams, the Welsh international, out of the side. However, his real success came when he replaced the injured Fred Kean at right-half during Wednesday's 1925–26 second division championship campaign. After appearing in 116 league and Cup games for the Owls, he went to Spurs in 1927 in the deal that brought Jimmy Seed to Hillsborough. Lowdell had once been rejected by the North London club as being too small!

LOWEST. The lowest number of goals scored by Sheffield Wednesday in a single league season is 28 in 1919–20 when the club finished bottom of the first division and were relegated. The club's lowest points record in the League occurred in 1974–75 when the Owls gained just 21 points and were relegated to the third division for the first time in their history.

LYALL, JACK. Joining Wednesday from Jarrow, the 6ft 2in goalkeeper got his chance in the side following Frank Stubbs's performance in the 6–1 defeat at Notts County, when the Sheffield keeper, who had been kicked in the head, presented their opponents with all six goals. Lyall became a permanent fixture in the Wednesday goal, winning league championship medals in 1902–03 and 1903–04. In 1905, the Dundee-born goalkeeper won his only full cap for Scotland, in the 1–0 defeat against England at Crystal Palace. After playing on the losing side in two FA Cup finals, he finally got a winners' medal in 1907 when Wednesday beat Everton 2–1. Lyall played in 295 games for the Owls before losing his place to Teddy Davison in 1909. He joined Manchester

City but returned to Hillsborough during the First World War, guesting for Wednesday in 19 games.

LYONS, MIKE. Croxteth-born Mike Lyons made his league debut for Everton in March 1971, scoring one of the goals in a 3–2 defeat at Nottingham Forest. He went on to build a brilliant career for himself at Goodison Park, appearing in 460 league and

Mike Lyons

Cup games. Sadly, despite dedicating the best years of his life to a club he dearly loved, he won nothing during his time with the Toffees. In August 1982, he severed his ties with the club and joined Sheffield Wednesday. A natural choice as captain, he led the Owls to the semi-finals of the FA Cup in 1982–83 and the following season was an ever-present as the club finally won promotion back to the first division. In November 1985, he became Grimsby Town's player–coach but was sacked in June 1987 after they were relegated. A month later, he rejoined Everton as reserve-team coach. Dismissed following the appointment of Howard Kendall, he was later appointed first-team coach at Wigan Athletic.

M

McANEARNEY, JIM. Arriving at Hillsborough with his brother Tom, Jim made his league debut for Wednesday in a 1–1 draw at home to Liverpool in February 1954. Facing stiff competition for an inside-forward berth from Froggatt, Sewell and Quixall, his appearances for the Owls were restricted to 40 league and Cup games over six seasons. When Wednesday were relegated to the second division in 1957–58, McAnearney scored three goals in the first four games of the season but still failed to hold down a regular place. He scored three goals in 11 appearances the following season as the club returned to the top flight but in January 1960, he joined Plymouth Argyle. He played in 135 league games for the Home Park club, later playing for Watford and Bradford City. After a spell as manager of Rotherham United, he returned to Hillsborough as first-team coach when Steve Burtenshaw was manager. When Burtenshaw was sacked, McAnearney had a short period in charge of team affairs before finding himself surplus to requirements.

McANEARNEY, TOM. Joining Sheffield Wednesday in 1950 from Dundee St Stephen's, Tom McAnearney made his debut for the Owls in the match against Liverpool at Hillsborough in September 1952. However, he had to wait until the following season before establishing himself in the side. Though he was never an ever-present, he played in 382 league and Cup matches for the Owls over the next 13 seasons, scoring 22 goals. Many of his goals were from the penalty spot, including two during the club's run to the FA Cup semi-finals in 1959–60. Having helped Wednesday to win the second division championship in 1955–56 and 1958–59, the constructive wing-half captained the club for a short spell during the early 1960s. In November 1965, he left to join Peterborough United and after only a few months became player–manager at Aldershot, where he played in 106 league games. In 1968 he returned to Hillsborough as coach, later as acting manager following Jack Marshall's sacking. In November 1970 he took over as Bury's manager, returning to Aldershot in May 1972. He was at the Recreation Ground for nine years, leading the Shots to promotion to division three on goal average in his first season.

McCALLIOG, JIM. When the Glasgow-born inside-forward joined Wednesday from Chelsea for £37,500 in October 1965, he became the country's costliest teenager. At the end of that season, he had helped the club reach the FA Cup final and scored the first goal in the 3–2 defeat by Everton. He was capped five times by Scotland and on his international debut scored in a 3–2 win against England at Wembley. He had scored 27 goals in 174 appearances for the Owls when he became unsettled and joined Wolverhampton Wanderers for £70,000. After scoring 34 goals in 163 league appearances for the Molineux club, he had a spell with Manchester United before joining Southampton. A member of the FA Cup winning side of 1976, he left two years later, ending his career with Lincoln City.

McCULLOCH, ANDY. Starting League football late, Andy McCulloch joined Queens Park Rangers from Walton and Hersham in 1970. When he signed for Wednesday in June 1979, he had played for Cardiff, Oxford and Brentford, scoring 91 league goals in 258 appearances. A tall, well-built forward, he scored on his debut on the opening day of the 1979–80 season in a 3–0 win at Barnsley. With 12 goals in 30 games that season, he helped the Owls win promotion. In 1980–81, McCulloch was the club's top scorer with 18 goals in 39 league games including a hat-trick in a 4–1 win over Cambridge United. He remained at

Hillsborough until the summer of 1983 when he joined Crystal Palace. He had scored 49 goals in 149 games and was one of the bravest strikers to have played for the club. In November 1984, he left Selhurst Park and ended his career with Aldershot.

McEVOY, DON. Don McEvoy began his career with Huddersfield Town, making 148 league appearances for the Terriers before joining Wednesday for £15,000 in December 1954. Making his debut in a 2–2 draw against Wolverhampton Wanderers, McEvoy proved to be a dependable player over the next four seasons, although he was unable to prevent the Owls from being relegated in his first season. In 1955–56 he was appointed captain and led Wednesday to the second division championship. His only goal for the club in 112 first-team appearances came the following season in the first division when he netted in the 4–2 defeat at Manchester City. He left Hillsborough in 1958 to play for Lincoln City, later playing for Barrow. He then had a spell as coach at Halifax before returning to Holker Street to become Barrow's manager. He led them to promotion, later managing Grimsby Town and Southport.

McINTOSH, DAVE. Scottish-born goalkeeper Dave McIntosh joined Wednesday in October 1947 and made his debut in a 2–0 win at Fulham in April 1948, after being third choice behind Morton and Smith. The following season he was an ever-present and again in 1951–52 when Wednesday won the second division championship. He began to suffer a series of injuries, including breaking his arm twice in the space of 12 months. There is no doubt had he been able to steer clear of these mishaps, he would have made many more than the 308 first-team appearances he is credited with. In January 1958, he joined Doncaster Rovers, playing his last game in English football for Rovers against Wednesday in a County Cup match at Hillsborough the following year.

McINTYRE, JOHNNY. After joining Wednesday from Fulham in March 1920, left-half Johnny McIntyre was converted into a centre-forward the following September. In 1920–21 in the game against Birmingham, he had just scored from the penalty spot when he was sent off after retaliating to the rough treatment he

105

was receiving. On his return to the side, he moved to inside-left to accommodate Sam Taylor and ended the season with 27 goals in 41 games, including a hat-trick against Coventry City. Halfway through the following season, he was rather surprisingly allowed to leave and join Blackburn Rovers. Though he later played for Blackpool, it was with the Ewood Park club that he made his name. On 16 September 1922, he scored four goals in five minutes as Rovers beat Everton 5–1.

McLEAN, DAVID. Born in Forfar, David McLean played his early football with his home-town club and Glasgow Celtic before moving south of the border to play for Preston North End. After scoring 24 goals in 49 appearances for the Deepdale club, he joined Wednesday in February 1911 for a fee of £1,000. In 1911–12, McLean topped Wednesday's goalscoring charts with 25 in 37 league games, including four goals in an 8–0 Boxing Day win over Sunderland and a hat-trick in the final game of the season, a 5–1 win at West Bromwich Albion. The following season, he won his only cap for Scotland when he played against England at Stamford Bridge, partnering Andrew Wilson. It was a good season for McLean who set a club record with 30 goals in the League, plus eight in the FA Cup. His tally including four in the 5–1 first-round win over Grimsby Town and a hat-trick in the 6–0 defeat of Chelsea in a second-round replay. Though he failed to net a hat-trick in the League, he did score nine doubles. At the end of that 1912–13 season, McLean had a disagreement with the club over terms and returned north of the border to play in Scottish junior football. However, in January 1914 he returned to Hillsborough on the original terms. In 1914–15 he scored another hat-trick in the 6–0 beating of Bradford and again ended the season as top scorer with 22 goals in 33 games. During the war, he guested for Third Lanark and Glasgow Rangers but when the hostilities were over, he played in a further three games for the club before joining Bradford. Later managing East Fife, McLean scored exactly 100 league and Cup goals in only 147 matches for Wednesday.

McMULLAN, JIMMY. Scottish-born Jimmy McMullan played his early football with Partick Thistle and was a great captain for both club and country, for whom he won 16 caps. However, he was desperate to move south and after a spell as player-manager of Maidstone United, he joined Manchester City. He made 242 appearances for the Maine Road club, gaining two FA Cup losers' medals in 1926 and 1933 and a second division championship medal in 1928. McMullan also captained the Wembley Wizards who beat England 5–1 in 1928. He began his managerial career with Oldham Athletic before having a brief spell with Aston Villa. He had been manager of Notts County for just over 12 months when he got the chance to take charge at Hillsborough. The Owls were near the foot of the second division when he arrived at the club in December 1937 but under his leadership their fortunes improved and they pulled clear of the danger zone. The following season, Wednesday were beaten to promotion by Sheffield United, who won their final game of the season to clinch promotion by one point from the Owls who finished third. His contract was not renewed in 1942.

MADDEN, LAWRIE. Preferring to concentrate on his studies, Lawrie Madden turned down the chance of joining Arsenal and got his first taste of league football as an amateur with Mansfield Town. After completing his degree in economics and social studies at Manchester University, he had a trial with Charlton Athletic and went on to appear in 113 league games before joining Millwall in March 1982. He had made 47 league appearances for the Lions before he moved to Hillsborough in August 1983. Immediately settling into the Wednesday back four, he was an important member of the side that won promotion from the second division. Over the next six seasons of top-flight football, Madden proved himself to be the most competent of defenders. At the end of the 1990–91 season, he left Hillsborough after appearing in 266 first-team games to sign for Wolverhampton Wanderers. After 76 games for the Molineux club, he played for Darlington and Chesterfield before concentrating on a career in sports journalism.

MANAGERS. This is the complete list of Wednesday's full-time managers with the inclusive dates during which they held office:

1920–33	Bob Brown	1971–73	Derek Dooley
1933–37	Billy Walker	1974–75	Steve Burtenshaw
1937–42	Jimmy McMullan	1975–77	Len Ashurst

1942–58	Eric Taylor	1977–83	Jack Charlton
1958–61	Harry Catterick	1983–88	Howard Wilkinson
1961–64	Vic Buckingham	1989	Peter Eustace
1964–68	Alan Brown	1989–91	Ron Atkinson
1968–69	Jack Marshall	1991–95	Trevor Francis
1969–71	Danny Williams	1995–	David Pleat

MARATHON MATCHES. During the 1978–79 season, Sheffield Wednesday were involved in five matches against Arsenal in the third round of the FA Cup. The Owls, then in the third division drew 1–1 at home to the first division outfit with Jeff Johnson scoring their goal. Rodger Wylde scored for Wednesday in the replay at Highbury which ended with a similar scoreline. Six days later at Filbert Street, former Arsenal player Brian Hornsby scored both Wednesday's goals in the fourth meeting which ended 3–3. Arsenal eventually won through to the fourth round with a 2–0 win in the fifth meeting of these two clubs in 17 days. Sheffield Wednesday only reached the 1890 FA Cup final after negotiating a problematic quarter-final tie with Notts County. At their first meeting which Wednesday won 5–0, Notts complained about the pitch and the game was replayed. This time Notts won 3–2 but it was Wednesday's turn to make a protest, this time about an ineligible player fielded by Notts. So the tie went to a third game which passed without incident and Wednesday won 2–1.

MARKSMEN – LEAGUE. Wednesday's top league goalscorer is Andrew Wilson who struck 199 League goals during his 20 years at Hillsborough. Only eight players have hit more than 100 league goals for the club:

1. Andrew Wilson   199
2. John Fantham   147
3. Redfern Froggatt   140
4. Mark Hooper   125
5. Ellis Rimmer   122
6. Jimmy Trotter   109
7. David Hirst   104
8. Fred Spiksley   100
9. Harry Chapman   94
10. Roy Shiner   93

MARKSMEN – OVERALL. Ten players have hit a century of goals for Sheffield Wednesday. The club's top marksman is Andrew Wilson. The Century Club consists of:

1. Andrew Wilson   216
2. John Fantham   162
3. Redfern Froggatt   149
4. Ellis Rimmer   140
5. Mark Hooper   136
6. David Hirst   126
7. Fred Spiksley   116
8. Jimmy Trotter   114
9. Harry Chapman   102
10. David McLean   100

MARRIOTT, JACK. Signed from Scunthorpe United, who were then members of the Midland League, for £2,000, Jack Marriott spent nine seasons at Hillsborough without ever really establishing himself. In 1949–50 when Wednesday won promotion from the second division, he played in 30 games and though he could operate on either flank, he preferred the right-wing. Yet competition was stiff and it was 1954–55 before he gained an extended run in the side, scoring seven goals in his last 21 appearances. However, at the end of that campaign, he was allowed to join Huddersfield Town after having scored 19 goals in 159 appearances for the Owls. In 1957 he returned to the Old Show Ground to end his career with Scunthorpe United, who by then had become members of the Football League.

MARSDEN, BILLY. Signed as an inside-forward from Sunderland in 1924, Billy Marsden made his debut at Crystal Palace in the opening game of the 1924–25 season and scored Wednesday's goal in their 1–0 win. Towards the end of that season, he switched to left-half with great success. He was an ever-present the following season when Wednesday won the second division championship and again in 1926–27. He won his first international cap for England against Wales in a 6–0 win at Stamford Bridge in 1929 and was playing in his third match for his country when a spinal injury ended his career. England were playing Germany in Berlin. It wasn't an opponent who was involved in the accident but Huddersfield Town's Roy Goodall who along with Marsden went for the same ball. Marsden tried hard to overcome the problem but after a handful of reserve games, he had to retire. He had a short spell as coach at Gateshead before becoming part-time manager of Doncaster Rovers.

MARSHALL, JACK. A player with Burnley before the war, Jack Marshall's career was cut short by injury and he joined the coaching staff at Bury. After a spell with Stoke City, he moved to Sheffield Wednesday as head trainer, a position he also held with the England B team. In September 1958, he moved to Spotland to become manager of Rochdale. He joined Blackburn Rovers six matches into the 1960–61 season and against all the odds, kept them challenging for the first division championship, playing entertaining football. After Marshall sold Fred Pickering, whom he'd converted to centre-forward, to Everton, the side began to break up and in 1965–66 were relegated. In February 1967, unhappy with several aspects of life at Ewood, Marshall tendered his resignation. He returned to football as Alan Brown's assistant at Hillsborough and when Brown and Wednesday parted company, Marshall became manager. A year later, he was told that his contract was not being renewed and he moved on to manage Bury. In July 1970, he returned to Ewood Park as physiotherapist, before finally retiring to his native Bolton in 1979.

MARWOOD, BRIAN. A skilful right-winger who had a good goalscoring record at Hull City, where he began his league career, Brian Marwood was soon attracting the attention of the bigger clubs and in August 1984, he joined Sheffield Wednesday for £115,000. He quickly made his mark in the first division after making his debut against Nottingham Forest at Hillsborough on the opening day of the 1984–85 season. The following season he was the club's leading goalscorer and when he was injured midway through the 1986–87 season, it coincided with one of the club's leanest spells. When he returned to first-team duty, he seemed to lack confidence and in March 1988 after scoring 35 goals in 160 first-team games for the Owls, he was transferred to Arsenal for £600,000. At Highbury, he won a league championship medal and his one and only England cap when he came on as substitute against Saudi Arabia. Following

Brian Marwood

the Gunners' recruitment of Anders Limpar, Marwood returned
to Sheffield, but this time to United. By now, he had been
appointed to the PFA and his appearances dwindled. After a loan
spell at Middlesbrough didn't work out, he joined Swindon

111

Town as a non-contract player before ending his league career with Barnet.

MASSEY, JIMMY. Goalkeeper Jimmy Massey joined Wednesday from Doncaster Rovers and kept a clean sheet on his debut as they beat Aston Villa 1–0 in November 1894. Though he played the odd game over the next season or so, his big chance came in January 1896 when he replaced the injured Bill Allen. He kept his place for the rest of the season and won an FA Cup winners' medal as Wednesday beat Wolves 2–1 to win the trophy for the first time. He was an ever-present in 1896–97, keeping 12 clean sheets in his 30 appearances, and went on to appear in a total of 173 games in a Wednesday career that spanned seven years. Massey won a second division championship medal in 1899–1900 but after sustaining a bad injury in the match against Bury in January 1901, he was forced to give up the game.

MEGSON, DON. Don Megson arrived at Hillsborough from Cheshire league side Mossley in October 1952 as an outside-left but for the next seven seasons played in almost every other position for the reserve side. When Harry Catterick arrived, he decided Megson's best position was left-back and gave him his League debut at home to Burnley in November 1959. In 1960, he represented the Football League against the Italian League and the following season was an ever-present, as he was in seasons 1963–64, 1964–65 and 1966–67. He played in 119 consecutive league games between 1 December 1962 and 23 October 1965. Replacing Tom McAnearney as captain, Megson skippered the Owls to the FA Cup final of 1966, taking the team on a losers' lap of honour at Wembley. He had played in 442 league and Cup games for Wednesday when he joined Bristol Rovers as player–coach. He later took over as manager and almost immediately, Rovers won the Watney Cup. In 1974 they gained promotion to division two but in 1977 he left Eastville to coach Portland Timbers in the NASL. Later he was manager of Bournemouth.

MEGSON, GARY. The son of former Sheffield Wednesday captain Don Megson, Gary made his league debut for Plymouth Argyle against Portsmouth in October 1977. He spent two seasons with the Home Park club before joining Everton for £250,000, a figure that broke Argyle's transfer record. He was brought to Hillsborough by Jack Charlton in August 1981 for £130,000 and made his debut against Blackburn Rovers on the opening day of the 1981–82 season. He missed only three league games in three seasons with the Owls and was an ever-present in 1983–84 when he helped the club win promotion from the second division. He joined Nottingham Forest but after three months without a game, was sold to Newcastle United, who were then managed by Jack Charlton. When Charlton left St James' Park, Megson was left in the cold and jumped at the chance to return to Wednesday for a second spell. He stayed for another three years during which he developed into a great team man before being allowed to join Manchester City, where he marked his debut by scoring the only goal of the game against Oldham Athletic. He helped the club win promotion and was a key figure in midfield as City consolidated their position in the top flight. In the summer of 1992 he was given a free transfer and joined Norwich City, becoming their caretaker manager for the last five games of the 1994–95 season. He played on a non-contract basis for Lincoln and Shrewsbury before being appointed first-team coach at Bradford City. Now manager of Stockport County after a spell in charge at Blackpool, he appeared in 286 first-team games for Wednesday in his two spells with the club.

MELLING, FRANK. Though he never played in a league or Cup game for Wednesday, Frank Melling enjoyed two very successful seasons with the club during the Second World War. He scored on his debut in a 1–1 draw at home to Lincoln City in September 1941 and in 55 appearances scored 35 goals, including hat-tricks against Rotherham United and Chesterfield and four goals against Nottingham Forest, all in the 1942–43 season. At the end of that season, he played in both legs of the League North War Cup final when Wednesday were beaten 4–3 on aggregate by Blackpool. He went to University to study architecture and captained the UAU in 1947. He also played for the English Universities XI against Scotland and appeared in an amateur international trial. Wednesday wanted him to turn out in their second division side after the war, but Melling refused. In 1954 he became a director of Sheffield United and served on the Bramall Lane club's board for over 25 years.

MIDLAND LEAGUE. Sheffield Wednesday reserves won the midland league championship in 1902–03, 1905–06, 1907–08 and 1922–23. In their first season as champions, they also won the Sheffield Challenge Cup and the Wharncliffe Charity Cup.

MILK CUP. See Football League Cup

MILLERSHIP, WALTER. Signed from Bradford for £2,750 in 1930, Walter Millership's early opportunities at Hillsborough were limited, though when he was given an extended run in 1931–32, he showed his abilities with 14 goals in 17 games, including a hat-trick in a 5–1 win over Blackburn Rovers and four goals in the 7–0 FA Cup triumph over Bournemouth. However, his best years with Wednesday were when he was switched to centre-half and replaced Tony Leach. He was an ever-present in 1934–35 and played his part in the club's winning of the FA Cup that season. Nicknamed 'Battleship', the ex-Nottinghamshire miner went on to make over 150 appearances for the Owls during the Second World War and played an important role in Wednesday's run to the League North War Cup final in 1943.

Walter Millership

MIROCEVIC, ANTE. Signed from Buducnost in September 1980, Mirocevic cost a club record fee of £200,000. Great things were expected of the Yugoslavian international, yet he was probably the most disappointing of all Jack Charlton's signings during his time as manager. He scored the Owls' second goal in the 2–2 home draw with Orient on his debut, but failed to live up to the hopes of Wednesday supporters. He appeared in only 70 first-team games during his three seasons at Hillsborough, but in 1982–83 helped the club to the semi-final of the FA Cup. He scored Wednesday's goal in the 2–1 defeat at Highbury against Brighton. Shortly afterwards, he returned to Yugoslavia on a free transfer.

MOBLEY, VIC. Joining Sheffield Wednesday from his home-town club, Oxford City, Vic Mobley made his first-team debut at Wolverhampton Wanderers in April 1964, following the events that led to the end of England international Peter Swan's first division career. In 1964–65, Mobley was an ever-present and won the first of 13 England Under-23 caps when he played against Wales. The following season, he was injured in the FA Cup semi-final against Chelsea and played for an hour with damaged ankle ligaments. Unfortunately he had not recovered in sufficient time to take part in the 1966 final against Everton. However, he soon got over that disappointment and went on to appear in 123 consecutive league and Cup games before joining Queens Park Rangers in October 1969 for £55,000. He played in just 25 League games for the Loftus Road club before knee trouble forced him to retire.

MOSFORTH, WILLIE. In the days when players could play for several clubs, Willie Mosforth would often play for Wednesday and Sheffield Albion on the same day. In fact, on one occasion, he was due to play against Wednesday, but because a supporter offered him money to play for Wednesday, he changed his shirt minutes before the kick-off and turned out for the Owls. He joined Wednesday in 1877 and made the first of his nine appearances for England against Scotland later that year, aged 19. Two years later, he was carried off shoulder high after dominating England's 5–4 victory over the Scots at the Kennington Oval. In 1882, he played in both semi-final matches of the FA Cup against Blackburn Rovers and two internationals against Scotland and Wales, all in the space of ten days. He left Wednesday in 1889 to join newly formed rivals, Sheffield United.

MOST MATCHES. Sheffield Wednesday played their most number of matches, 59, in 1978–79. This comprised 46 league games, nine FA Cup games and four League Cup games.

MULLEN, JIMMY. Jimmy Mullen made his Wednesday debut in a remarkable 4–4 draw at Hull City on Boxing Day 1970 and though the majority of his games were played in the third division following the club's relegation in 1974–75, he proved himself to be a more than capable defender. He played the last of his 262 first-team games as a substitute in March 1980, helping the Owls win promotion to the second division. He joined Ian Porterfield at Rotherham United before signing for Cardiff City in March 1982, where he played in 133 league games for the Ninian Park club. After hanging up his boots, he became Alan Durban's assistant, later rejoining Porterfield at Aberdeen.

MUMFORD, ALBERT. Shropshire-born Albert Mumford came to Sheffield in 1881 and played for Bethel United and Bethel Reds before helping both Wednesday and Lockwood Brothers as an amateur. One of the great Wednesday favourites of the Olive Grove period, he turned professional and played in every position on the field, including goalkeeper. His debut between the sticks against Sunderland Albion only saw him beaten by a penalty-kick. However, it was as a dashing forward that 'Clinks' as he became known, made his name. He was at his best in 1889–90 when Wednesday won the Alliance Championship and reached the FA Cup final for the first time in their history. He scored both goals in the semi-final when Wednesday beat Bolton Wanderers 2–1 and some even claimed that Wednesday's goal in the 6–1 final defeat by Blackburn Rovers came from his head and not Bennett's.

N

NAPIER, CHARLIE. Scottish international inside-forward Charlie Napier began his professional career with Celtic, playing for the Parkhead club between 1929 and 1935. The club refused to grant the popular player a benefit and so he came south of the border to join Derby County. Dubbed 'Happy Feet' by the Baseball Ground faithful, he played in 88 games for the Rams before Jimmy McMullan signed him for Wednesday in March 1938. In 1938–39 he missed just one game, as the Owls finished third in division two, missing promotion by just one point. Not a prolific goalscorer, he netted nine goals in his 41 appearances, including a hat-trick in a 4–3 defeat at Southampton. He scored two in the 3–1 victory over Barnsley in August 1939 but one game later, war was declared and league football stopped. Following an incident in the match at home to Grimsby Town in October 1943, Napier was banned *sine die* and though the ban was later lifted, his career in England was finished. He returned to Scotland to end his playing days with Falkirk.

Charlie Napier

NEUTRAL GROUNDS. Hillsborough has been used as a neutral ground for 32 FA Cup semi-finals from 1912 to 1997 and as early as 1920, staged the England v Scotland international. Unfortunately, heavy rain and local unemployment kept the attendance down to 25,536 but those who did turn up, saw England come from behind to win 5–4. In 1950, Hillsborough was, for the first time, the venue for an England B international against Switzerland and a year later staged its first inter-league game. In 1962, Hillsborough was chosen as the venue for England's European Nations international against France which ended 1–1. When England were selected to host the 1966 World Cup, Hillsborough was an obvious choice for group matches. In 1973, Hillsborough staged the Northern Ireland v Bulgaria international. In 1977, Aston Villa and Everton replayed their League Cup final and in 1996, four European Championship matches were played at the ground. Sheffield Wednesday have also had to replay on a neutral ground a number of times:

Date	Opponents	Venue	FA Cup	Score
25.01.39	Chester	Maine Road	Rd 4 2R	2–0
20.02.39	Chelsea	Highbury	Rd 5 2R	1–3
14.01.57	Preston North End	Goodison Park	Rd 3 2R	1–5
19.02.73	Crystal Palace	Villa Park	Rd 4 2R	3–2
15.01.79	Arsenal	Filbert Street	Rd 3 2R	2–2
17.01.79	Arsenal	Filbert Street	Rd 3 3R	3–3
22.01.79	Arsenal	Filbert Street	Rd 3 4R	0–2

The club's semi-finals were of course played on neutral grounds:

Date	Opponents	Venue	Score
10.03.1894	Bolton Wanderers	Fallowfield	1–2
16.03.1895	West Bromwich Albion	Derby	0–2
21.03.1896	Bolton Wanderers	Goodison Park	1–1
26.03.1896	Bolton Wanderers	Nottingham	3–1
19.03.04	Manchester City	Goodison Park	0–3
25.03.05	Newcastle United	Hyde Road	0–1
23.03.07	Woolwich Arsenal	St Andrews	3–1
22.03.30	Huddersfield Town	Old Trafford	1–2
16.03.35	Burnley	Villa Park	3–0
27.03.54	Preston North End	Maine Road	0–2
26.03.60	Blackburn Rovers	Maine Road	1–2
23.04.66	Chelsea	Villa Park	2–0

16.04.83	Brighton & Hove Albion	Highbury	1–2
05.04.86	Everton	Villa Park	1–2
03.04.93	Sheffield United	Wembley	2–1

The club's FA Cup final appearances at Crystal Palace and Wembley also qualify as does the Owls' appearance at the home of football in the League Cup final.

NIBLOE, JOE. Beginning his career with Kilmarnock, Joe Nibloe won a Scottish Cup winners' medal in 1929, the year that he won the first of his 11 Scottish caps when he played against England in Glasgow. In the summer of 1932, he joined Aston Villa for a fee of £1,800 but within two years, he had signed for Wednesday in the part-exchange deal which took George Beeson to Villa Park. A tough-tackling full-back, he made his Wednesday debut in the 4–1 home win over Stoke City on the opening day of the 1934–35 season. He went on to appear in 128 first-team games before losing his place to Albert Ashley during the 1937–38 season. He remained at Hillsborough until the outbreak of war, returning after the hostilities to coach Wednesday's junior sides.

Joe Nibloe

NICKNAMES. Sheffield Wednesday's nickname is the Owls. Many players in the club's history have been fondly known by their nicknames. They include:

Albert Mumford	1889–1894	'Clinks'
Harry Davis	1900–1907	'Joe Pluck'
Arthur Lowdell	1922–1927	'Darkie'
Walter Millership	1930–1939	'Battleship'
Charlie Tomlinson	1944–1951	'Shadow'
Norman Curtis	1950–1960	'Cannonball'
Mel Sterland	1979–1989	'Zico'

NICOL, STEVE. Before moving south to join Liverpool, Steve Nicol spent two seasons with Ayr United, where he impressed at full-back after signing from a local boy's club. After waiting almost 12 months for his league debut, he earned a more permanent place in the Liverpool side in 1983–84 and ended the season with league championship and European Cup winners' medals. Alternating between full-back and midfield, he scored his only hat-trick in Liverpool's 4–1 win at Newcastle United in September 1987. The following season he was switched to the centre of defence, because of injuries to Gillespie and Hansen, and was voted the Football Writers' Association Footballer of the Year in 1989. He made the first of his 27 appearances for Scotland in a 6–1 victory over Yugoslavia in 1984. After winning four league championship medals, three FA Cup winners' medals and a European Cup winners' medal with Liverpool, he joined Notts County on a free transfer in January 1995, playing in 34 games for the Meadow Lane club. He moved on to Sheffield Wednesday and made his debut in the game against Everton in November 1995. Initially seen as a short-term attempt to add experience to a Wednesday side struggling in the Premiership, Steve Nicol at the age of 35, is still a vital member of the Owls squad. He has played in a variety of positions.

NILSSON, ROLAND. A Swedish international full-back, Nilsson was signed by Sheffield Wednesday from IFK Gothenburg in December 1989 for £375,000 to fill the gap at right-back that Mel Sterland's transfer to Rangers had created. Though he missed only one game in 1989–90 after making his debut against Luton Town, he couldn't prevent the Owls being relegated. The following season, Wednesday were undefeated in their first 14 games and were leading 2–0 at Millwall when Nilsson was injured; they proceded to lose 4–2. Nilsson was out of the side until April when he returned to help the club win promotion and appeared in the League Cup final, when Wednesday beat Manchester United 1–0. He starred for Sweden in the 1992 European Championship when the host country reached the semi-finals before losing to Germany. One of the best right-backs in the Premiership, he made 181 first-team appearances before leaving the club at the end of the 1993–94 season.

120

NOLAN, IAN. Liverpool-born full-back Ian Nolan joined Preston North End after leaving school, but having failed to make the grade at Deepdale, he moved to non-league Northwich Victoria before signing for Marine. Then in the summer of 1991, Tranmere Rovers secured his services for £10,000 and he went on to play in 105 first team games for the Prenton Park club before moving to Wednesday for £1.5 million in August 1994. An ever-present in 1994–95, his first season at the club, he played in both full-back positions in the following season and had made 83 consecutive league and Cup appearances before injuring ligaments in a 3–2 defeat at Aston Villa. Back to his best in 1996–97, Nolan has given the Wednesday side better balance and more attacking options.

NON-LEAGUE. Non-league is the term used for clubs which are not members of the Football League. On 19 January 1920, Darlington, then members of the North Eastern League beat Sheffield Wednesday 2–0 and so became the first non–league club to win on a division one ground in the FA Cup competition. However, despite that setback, the Owls have a good record against non-league clubs in the FA Cup. The club's record since that defeat at the hands of Darlington is:

Date	Opponents	Venue	Result
13.01.23	New Brighton Tower	Home	Won 3–0
07.01.39	Yeovil Town	Home	Drew 1–1
12.01.39	Yeovil Town	Away	Won 2–1
08.01.55	Hastings United	Home	Won 2–1
04.01.58	Hereford United	Away	Won 3–0
30.01.60	Peterborough United	Home	Won 2–0
22.11.75	Macclesfield Town	Home	Won 3–1
13.12.75	Wigan Athletic	Home	Won 2–0
17.12.77	Wigan Athletic	Away	Lost 0–1

O

O'DONNELL, RALPH. A dependable centre-half, Ralph O'Donnell was doing his National Service in the RAF when he made his league debut for Wednesday in a 2–1 win over Bury in November 1951. Despite fracturing his cheekbone in his third game against Coventry City, he played in 13 games to help Wednesday win the second division championship. Towards the end of 1953, he broke his leg and after losing his place to Don McEvoy, reverted to defensive wing-half with great success. In 1955–56, he helped Wednesday win the second division championship for a fourth time and scored his first goal for the club in a 4–0 win over Port Vale. In 1958 he switched to part-time professional as he trained to become a teacher and played the last of his 183 first-team games in 1961. He left Hillsborough three years later, becoming a notable figure in schoolboy football.

OLDEST PLAYER. The oldest player to line-up in a Sheffield Wednesday team is Tom Brittleton. He was 41 years old when he played his last game for the club against Oldham Athletic (home 1–0) on 1 May 1920.

OLIVE GROVE. Rented from the Duke of Norfolk's estate, Olive Grove was a swampy field, cut across by a brook and a footpath. The Midland Railway line between Sheffield and Heeley stations ran within yards of the northern touchline. The club elected to spend around £5,000 in turning this swampy field into a decent ground. A stand with 1,000 seats was built, the brook culverted and iron railings erected around the pitch. The first match on the ground took place on 12 September 1887, when a crowd of barely 2,000 saw Wednesday take on the FA Cup holders Blackburn Rovers. During the club's run to the FA Cup final in 1896, where they beat Wolverhampton Wanderers 2–1, a record home attendance of 28,000 witnessed the 4–0 defeat of Everton in round three. Funded by the club's success that season, a main stand was built on the Olive Grove side. It was at Olive Grove that the abandoned match against Aston Villa took place. Bad light stopped play after 79 minutes with Wednesday leading 3–1 but rather than let the result stand, the League ordered the remaining 11 minutes to be played at a later date. So on 13 March 1899, the shortest-ever football league match took place at Olive Grove with Wednesday scoring another goal to win 4–1. However, a month earlier, the club's lease at Olive Grove had expired and instead of being renewed as they had expected, they were ordered to leave by the end of the season. The last few weeks at Olive Grove were not happy ones. On 15 April 1899, only 4,000 turned up to see Wednesday play their last game at the ground. They lost 3–1 to Newcastle United and were relegated. Since the club's departure, the site has been occupied by a council works depot. In 1995, a plaque was unveiled to commemorate Wednesday's 12 years at the ground.

OVERSEAS PLAYERS. One of the first overseas players to join the club was Yugoslavian international Ante Mirocevic, who joined the club from Buducnost in September 1980 for a club record fee of £200,000. He never lived up to expectations and after making 70 appearances in three years at Hillsborough, returned to Yugoslavia on a free transfer. Icelandic international Siggi Jonsson was the next overseas player to arrive at Hillsborough, followed by Sweden's Roland Nilsson, signed from IFK Gothenburg for £375,000. He went on to be one of the best full-backs in the top flight before leaving Hillsborough at the end of the 1993–94 season. Australian international midfielder Adam Poric joined Wednesday in October 1993 but has struggled to make an impact in the English game. Romanian star Dan Petrescu joined the

Owls from Genoa in the summer of 1994 but became unsettled at Hillsborough and moved to Chelsea in November 1995. Also around this time, Wednesday signed Klas Ingesson, but the Swedish international was unable to adapt to the Premier League and moved to Italian side, Bari. Belgian star, Marc Degryse signed for the Owls from Anderlecht in August 1995 for £1.5 million and impressed in the one season he stayed with the club. The club's current overseas players include Yugoslavian international defender Dejan Stefanovic and Italian Benito Carbone. Other players with foreign-sounding surnames include Sam Chedgzoy, Len Massarella, Peter Rodrigues and Imre Varadi – all born in the British Isles.

OWLS. During the club's Olive Grove era, Wednesday were always known as The Blades, but became known as the Owls following their move to Owlerton in 1899. The nickname is artificial for the district is not pronounced Owlerton, but 'Olerton'.

OWN GOALS. On Boxing Day 1952, Sheffield Wednesday lost 5–4 to West Bromwich Albion at Hillsborough in front of a 59,389 crowd. In a remarkable game, both Norman Curtis and Eddie Gannon put the ball into their own net.

P

PACKARD, EDGAR. Signed from Clipstone in 1936, Edgar Packard did not make his league debut for the Owls for another ten years, though he did appear in 24 wartime games when on leave from service in the Italian and North African campaigns. He made his league debut in a 4–2 defeat at the hands of Barnsley. In that first season of league football after the war, he played in 29 games. Though he later fell out of favour, he was an ever-present in 1949–50 when Wednesday gained promotion to the first division. It was during this season when Wednesday beat West Ham United 2–1, that Packard scored his only goal for the club. Carrying the ball from his own penalty area, he took a return pass from Jordan before shooting past a bemused Hammers keeper. The following season he suffered a fractured jaw and in 1952 joined Halifax Town.

PALETHORPE, JACK. A native of Leicester, he started his footballing career with Maidenhead in the Spartan League and was on Crystal Palace's books for one season as an amateur. He was introduced to league football by Reading and scored 23 goals in 1931–32 and 29 the following season before signing for Stoke City. He helped the Potters to promotion before moving to Preston North End in January 1934. He arrived at Hillsborough in December 1934 and on Boxing Day scored a hat-trick in the

Owls' 4–0 win at Birmingham. That season he played in all five games in the club's run to the FA Cup final, scoring three goals. In the final, his early goal settled Wednesday's nerves and they went on to beat West Bromwich Albion 4–2. In 1935–36, he scored five goals in the first eight matches before signing for Aston Villa. He was one of a number of players signed by the Villa Park club in a desperate bid to avoid relegation. Unable to prevent the Villans dropping into the second division, he returned to Crystal Palace.

PALMER, CARLTON. Having made his league debut for West Bromwich Albion in September 1985, Carlton Palmer continued to hold down a regular place until his former boss Ron Atkinson signed him for Sheffield Wednesday for £750,000 in February 1989. Despite settling down well at Hillsborough in his first full season, he couldn't prevent the Owls from being relegated to the second division. However, he only missed two matches in 1990–91 as Wednesday finished in third place to win promotion at the first time of asking. Unfortunately injury ruled him out of the Wednesday side that won the League Cup that season. In 1991–92, he was an ever-present

Carlton Palmer

and though not a prolific goalscorer, scored a first half hat-trick in a 4–1 win over Queens Park Rangers. Also that season he won the first of his 18 international caps against the CIS in Moscow. He was included in the England squad for the European Championship and was one of the few successes in a disappointing England performance. Confident and composed on the ball and equally at home at full-back, in central defence or in midfield, he had made 263 first-team appearances for the Owls when he was sold to Leeds United for £2.6 million in June 1994. A wholehearted member of the Leeds team, he has now played over 100 matches for the Elland Road club.

PEARSON, JOHN. Joining Wednesday straight from school, he made his debut against Bristol City in September 1980, scoring the opening goal in a 2–1 win. Despite showing a lot of promise, he was unable to command a regular place in the Wednesday side due to the likes of Bannister and Chapman, yet in the early 1980s, he gained both England Youth and Under-21 honours. During 1983–84, the lanky striker played in 27 of Wednesday's games as they won promotion from the second division. Yet when he left the club to join Charlton Athletic in May 1985, over a third of his 128 appearances were as a substitute. He helped Charlton win promotion to division one in his first season at the Valley but in January 1987 returned to Yorkshire to play for Leeds United. Again, at Elland Road many of his first-team appearances were as a substitute and after a loan spell at Rotherham United, he joined Barnsley. A loan stint at Hull City was followed by moves to Carlisle United, Mansfield Town and Cardiff City.

PEARSON, NIGEL. Pearson joined Shrewsbury Town from non-league side Heanor Town in November 1981 and had to wait nine months before making his League debut at Oldham Athletic. He had just won a regular place in the side when he was badly injured towards the end of the 1983–84 season and out of action for well over a year. He made a good recovery and was ever present during the 1986–87 season, impressing Wednesday's officials when Wednesday met Oldham in that season's League Cup competition. He signed for the Owls in October 1987 for a fee of £250,000 and rarely missed a game in those first few seasons. A player who inspires by example, he led the Owls to promotion from the second division and victory in the League Cup final in 1990–91, scoring 12 league and Cup goals, notably from free-kicks and corners. Frequently rested or absent through injury, he broke a leg in the 1992–93 League Cup semi-final at Blackburn. At the end of the following season after he had appeared in 224 first-team games for the club, he joined Middlesbrough for £500,000. Brave in the air and uncompromising on the ground, Pearson has missed few matches since leaving Hillsborough and as Boro's captain, has been a tower of strength in a side that has struggled in the lower reaches of the Premiership.

PEMBRIDGE, MARK. Welsh international Mark Pembridge began his league career with Luton Town but in June 1992 joined Derby County for £1.25 million. His impressive performances at the Baseball Ground, where he appeared in 140 games, led to a number of Premier League clubs chasing his services and in July 1995, Sheffield Wednesday brought him to Hillsborough for £900,000. He scored the winner in his second game for the Owls to give them a 2–1 victory over Blackburn Rovers but after that, in those early games, he struggled to make a real impact. However, he bounced back and was just starting to make an impression when he suffered a bad leg injury at Highbury. Never a regular scorer from midfield, there was a period in 1996–97 when he scored five goals in four consecutive games and Wednesday fans will hope that this small, combative midfielder continues to produce this kind of form.

PENALTIES. In the FA Cup match of 1908–09 against second division Glossop, Wednesday's left-back, Harry Burton, conceded the penalty that gave their opponents their goal and then missed one at the other end that would have levelled the scores. In the 1931–32 season, Jack Ball scored 23 goals for Wednesday, 11 of them from the penalty spot – a feat which remained a football league record for some 40 years. A penalty expert with Wednesday, especially during the war years, Joe Cockcroft missed the first spot-kick he took after joining Sheffield United. In 1952–53, Norman Curtis established a reputation as a penalty-taker. After someone had placed the ball on the spot, he would run all the way from defence before blasting the ball into the net. Andy Blair is most certainly assured of a place in Sheffield Wednesday's records after scoring a unique hat-trick of penalties in the League Cup tie at home to Luton Town in November 1984 which the Owls won 4–2.

PENALTY SHOOT-OUT. When Wednesday played Wolverhampton Wanderers in the fourth round of the FA Cup at Hillsborough, they lost the chance of victory through a missed penalty. The replay at Molineux ended level at 1–1 after extra-time. In the ensuing penalty shoot-out, the Owls went three up but completely lost their nerve as Wolves came back to gain one of the most outrageous victories ever in a penalty shoot-out.

PETRESCU, DAN. Signed from Italian club Genoa for £1.25 million in June 1994, the talented right-sided wing-back scored for Wednesday on his debut on the opening day of the 1994–95 season in a 4–3 home defeat against Spurs. In fact, his other goals that season were also against London clubs, as he helped beat West Ham United 1–0 and Arsenal 3–1. Having appeared in 41 league and Cup games, he became unsettled and uncertain of a first-team place at Hillsborough and after protracted transfer negotiations, signed for Chelsea for £2.3 million. An automatic choice for Romania over the last few seasons, he appeared in Euro '96 and in a short time at Stamford Bridge has become a great crowd favourite.

PICKERING, MIKE. After starting his career with Barnsley, the Mirfield-born defender joined Southampton, where he helped the Saints win promotion from the second division. He had played in 44 league games for the club from the Dell before signing for Wednesday in October 1978. He made his debut for the Owls in a 1–0 win at Rotherham United and after a number of impressive defensive displays, was chosen as club captain. In 1979–80 he played an important role in the Owls winning promotion from the third division, but in the seasons that followed, he was hampered by injuries and the improved form of Peter Shirtliff. Unable to command a regular first-team place, he had loan spells at Norwich City, Bradford City and Barnsley before joining Rotherham United in early 1984. He played in 102 league games for the Millmoor club before signing for York City. He later ended his career with Stockport County.

PITCH. The Hillsborough pitch measures 115 yards x 77 yards.

PLASTIC. Four league clubs replaced their normal grass playing pitches with artificial surfaces at one stage or another. Queens Park Rangers were the first in 1981 but the Loftus Road plastic was discarded in 1988 in favour of a return to turf. Luton Town (1985), Oldham Athletic (1986) and Preston North End (1986) followed. Wednesday never played on the Deepdale plastic but their results at the other three grounds were as follows:

	P	W	D	L	F	A
Queens Park Rangers	6	1	3	2	5	7
Luton Town	5	2	2	1	5	3
Oldham Athletic	2	0	0	2	2	6

Though Wednesday's record on plastic is not a good one, it is probably no worse than that of most clubs.

PLEAT, DAVID. A highly respected and innovative manager, David Pleat gained England Schoolboy and Youth honours before beginning his league career with Nottingham Forest. He played in only six games for the City Ground club before joining Luton Town for £8,000 in August 1964. During his first season with the Hatters, he broke his leg and thereafter moved around the lower divisions, playing for Shrewsbury Town, Exeter City and Peterborough United, making 184 league appearances. In 1971 he

David Pleat

joined Nuneaton Borough as player–manager, returning to Kenilworth Road as coach the following year. In 1978 he was promoted to manager and over the next eight seasons, established Luton as a first division club, renowned for attractive, attacking play, although in 1982–83 they only avoided relegation by winning their last game at Manchester City. Many will remember Pleat galloping across the Maine Road pitch to hug his players in delight. In May 1986 he joined Spurs and the following season took the club to third place in the first division and to the FA Cup final. It was Pleat who was responsible for the introduction of the style of play which used a five-man midfield in support of a lone front runner. However, early in the 1987–88 season, he resigned after lurid newspaper allegations about his private life. He soon accepted the manager's post at Leicester City but lost his job when the Filberts were nearly relegated in 1991. He returned to Kenilworth Road but in June 1995 he became manager of

Sheffield Wednesday. After an indifferent start to the 1995–96 season, Pleat moved into the transfer market in a big way, investing £4 million on Red Star Belgrade duo Darko Kovacevic and Dejan Stefanovic but neither was seen in action until Christmas. His side came perilously close to the drop, which was finally avoided on the last day of the season. There was a marked improvement in 1996–97 with Wednesday finishing in the top half of the table.

PLYMOUTH BOWL. After completing their 1902–03 league programme, the Owls travelled down to Devon to promote professional football in Plymouth. Playing for the Plymouth Bowl, they beat Notts County at Home Park 2–0 with goals from Malloch and Ruddlesdin. The destiny of the league championship was decided on that day, because Sunderland, who could have overtaken Wednesday had they won their last game at Newcastle, failed to do so, thus bringing the title to Owlerton.

POINTS. Under the three points for a win system which was introduced in 1981–82, Sheffield Wednesday's best points tally was 88 in 1983–84 when the club finished runners-up in the second division. However, the club's best points haul under the old two points for a win system was 62 in 1958–59 when they won the second division championship. This would have netted them 90 points under the present system. Wednesday's worst record under either system was the meagre 21 points secured in 1974–75 when the club were relegated to the third division for the first time in their history.

PROPHETT, COLIN. Signed as an amateur in September 1967, Colin Prophett made his first-team debut for Wednesday as a substitute for Alan Warboys in a 1–1 draw at home to Liverpool in August 1969. That season, when the Owls were relegated to the second division, he appeared in 30 games and was one of the few Wednesday players to come out of the season with any credit. Over the next two seasons, the tall centre-half was a regular and one of the best defenders in the second division. He missed just one game in 1971–72 but after losing his place the following season he joined Norwich City. After playing in 35 league games for the Carrow Road club, he signed for Swindon Town, where he played the best football of his career. He made 160 league appearances whilst at the County Ground before transferring to Chesterfield. He later ended his career with his home-town club, Crewe Alexandra.

PORTERFIELD, IAN. Beginning his career with Raith Rovers, Ian Porterfield joined Sunderland in 1967. Assured of a place in the Roker Park club's history after scoring the goal that gave the second division club a memorable FA Cup final victory over Leeds United, he went on to play in 230 league games for them before signing for Sheffield Wednesday in the summer of 1977. In 1974 he had been involved in a car crash and suffered a broken jaw and it was only his brave determination that allowed him to continue his career. An intelligent midfield player, he gave the Owls good service in the three years he was at the club. He left Hillsborough halfway through the promotion-winning season of 1979–80 to pursue a career in management with Rotherham United. He led the Millmoor club to the third division championship in 1980–81 and then left to take charge at Bramall Lane. He led the Blades from the fourth division to the second in three seasons. Yet, despite his good record with United, he was sacked. He was the surprise choice as Alex Ferguson's successor at Aberdeen, but despite leading the Dons to the semi-finals of the Scottish Cup and League Cup, he was dismissed. He then managed Reading, and despite little success, he was appointed manager of Chelsea in the summer of 1991. He lost his job again in February 1993 following a run of 12 games without a win.

POTTS, ERIC. Liverpool-born winger Eric Potts had a spell as an amateur with Blackpool before joining New Brighton and later Oswestry Town. He signed for Sheffield Wednesday in December 1969 and though he made 16 appearances (half of them as substitute) over the next three seasons, he had to wait until the 1973–74 season before winning a regular place in the first team. A quick and clever wide player, Potts was the club's only ever-present in the disastrous season of 1974–75 when the Owls slipped into the third division for the first time in their history. After scoring 25 goals in 182 league and Cup games, Potts was allowed to leave and joined Brighton and Hove

Albion. He later returned to his native Lancashire and played for Preston, Burnley and Bury before hanging up his boots.

POWELL, SAM. After playing junior football in his home town of Rotherham, Sam Powell began his league career with Leeds United, from where he joined Wednesday in March 1925. The Hillsborough club were near the foot of the second division when Powell arrived, but six goals in eight games, including a hat-trick in a 3–1 win against Fulham, helped Wednesday pull away from the relegation zone. Despite scoring in the opening game of the 1925–26 season, in which Wednesday won the second division championship, Powell did not keep his place. He was selected for the odd game, playing his last match for the Owls in March 1928. After hanging up his boots, Powell joined the club's backroom staff. He was appointed first team trainer in 1937 and stayed at the club until 1959.

PREMIER LEAGUE. With the shrewd acquisition of former England winger Chris Waddle from Marseilles for £1 million, Wednesday started 1992–93, the first season of the Premier League, well enough. It was Waddle's performances that were the mainstay of an assortment of individual feats during a season in which the Owls reached two Wembley finals and finished seventh in the Premier League. Waddle was voted the Football Writers' Association's Footballer of the Year. In the close season, Des Walker joined Wednesday from Sampdoria for £2 million and with the return of broken-leg victim Nigel Pearson and injured striker David Hirst, the situation looked quite promising. Yet after four games, the Owls had just one point and not one player able to find the net. There was a change in fortune in November after a 4–1 win at Ipswich and, despite an injury to Chris Waddle which ruled him out of the second half of the season, Wednesday finished seventh, the same as the previous season. In 1994–95, Hillsborough fans witnessed an entertaining start to the season, although the first two games were lost, 4–3 to Spurs and 3–2 to Queens Park Rangers. Two clean sheets followed but 4–1 defeats at Nottingham Forest and Liverpool shattered the illusion. Despite victories over Everton and Coventry over Christmas, the Owls embarked on a run of only three wins in 15 games, including a humiliating 7–1 defeat to Nottingham Forest at Hillsborough on April Fool's Day as they ended the season in 13th place. This slump in performances led to the dismissal of Trevor Francis and the appointment of David Pleat. After an indifferent start to the 1995–96 season, Pleat moved into the transfer market in a big way. He had signed Belgian captain Marc Degryse for £1.5 million in October and invested £4 million on Red Star Belgrade duo Dejan Stefanovic and Darko Kovacevic, though neither was seen in action until Christmas. After New Year, the Owls found goals hard to come by and were clearly on the slide. Jon Newsome was bought from Norwich City for £1.6 million to bolster the defence, but it was his goal in the 89th minute at Upton Park in the last game of the season that ensured Wednesday avoided the drop. In 1996–97, Wednesday won their first four league games and headed the Premier League, but though they couldn't maintain that form, they ended the season in seventh place, a much improved performance from previous years.

PRENDERGAST, MICK. After scoring on his league debut in a 3–2 defeat at Newcastle United on 9 April 1969, Mick Prendergast had to wait for a couple of seasons before winning a regular place. During that season of 1970–71, he was the Owls' top scorer with 16 goals. He was hampered by a series of injury problems, but in 1973–74, was voted 'Player of the Year' despite missing the last four games after breaking his leg at Preston North End. Earlier that season, his courage had brought him a hat-trick in a 4–0 win over Crystal Palace. After missing most of the following season, he ended the 1975–76 campaign as the club's top scorer before more injuries reduced his number of appearances. He stayed at Hillsborough until March 1978 when, after scoring 59 goals in 206 games, he joined Barnsley.

PRESSMAN, KEVIN. Goalkeeper Kevin Pressman was spotted by Sheffield Wednesday while playing for England Schoolboys and after working his way through the junior teams made his debut in a 1–1 draw at Southampton in September 1987. Replacing Martin Hodge towards the end of that season, he shared first-team duties with Chris Turner until 1989–90 when he played on a more regular basis. Unfortunately, he was stretchered off during the home game with Manchester City and didn't play again that season. The club were relegated to the second division. With the arrival of Chris Woods from Rangers, Pressman was loaned out to Stoke City for a short spell towards the end of the 1991–92 season. He remained in the shadow of Woods over the next couple of seasons before regaining his first-team place. A goalkeeper who excels in one-to-one situations, like most number ones, he fancies his chances as a striker, even more so after scoring in a penalty shoot-out against Wolves in 1994–95.

PROFESSIONALISM. The FA at first scorned professionalism and only accepted it in 1885, when they realised there was very little they could do about it. However, the FA Chairman, Charles Clegg, a Sheffield solicitor, was still opposed to the practice and the Wednesday committee supported his views. The club's attitude was difficult to understand, for in October 1876, they had brought James Lang from Scotland and given him a sinecure at the works of Walter Fearnehough, a member of the Wednesday committee. After Wednesday's entry for the 1886–87 FA Cup competition arrived too late, the matter of professionalism came to a head. A number of the club's players turned out for Lockwood Brothers and after they had been knocked out at the quarter-final stage of the competition, they decided to form their own professional club in the town, Sheffield Rovers. Fortunately, Wednesday realised that they could lose all their best players and so on 22 April 1887, the club agreed to turn professional.

PROMOTION. Sheffield Wednesday have been promoted on nine occasions and with the exception of 1979–80, always from the second division to the first. The Owls were first promoted in 1899–1900 in their first season at Owlerton, later to be called Hillsborough. They won all 17 of their home games, beating Luton Town 6–0, Burton Swifts 6–0, Chesterfield 5–1, Gainsborough Trinity 5–1, Barnsley 5–1 and Loughborough 5–0. Relegated in 1919–20, Wednesday's next promotion came in 1925–26 when they won the second division championship, finishing three points ahead of Derby County. Finishing bottom of the first division in 1936–37, Wednesday were next promoted in 1949–50 when they drew their final game at home to Spurs 0–0, to clinch promotion by 0.008 of a goal. After spending just one season in the top flight, Wednesday were relegated but bounced back immediately to win the second division championship in 1951–52, with Derek Dooley scoring 46 goals in 30 games. Relegated after three seasons in division one, the Owls won the second division championship again in 1955–56, scoring 101 goals as compared to exactly 100 when they won the League in 1951–52. Wednesday's sixth experience of promotion came in 1958–59 when they won the second division title for the third time in that decade. After 11 seasons in the first division, Wednesday were relegated in 1969–70 and in 1974–75 fell into the third division for the first time in their history. They won promotion to the second division in 1979–80, when an unbeaten run of 16 games starting in mid-January helped them finish third behind Grimsby Town and Blackburn Rovers. Wednesday returned to the first division in 1983–84, finishing level with Chelsea at the top on 88 points. The Owls dropped vital points in the final run-in and allowed the Stamford Bridge club to win the title on goal difference. The club's final experience of promotion came in 1990–91 when the Owls went up to the first division as the third-placed club behind Oldham Athletic and West Ham United.

PUGH, GRAHAM. Graham Pugh was 18 years old when he made his debut for the club against Tottenham Hotspur in April 1966. His first FA Cup tie came three games later when Wednesday beat Chelsea 2–0 in the semi-final at Villa Park and at the end of the season, he picked up a runners-up medal in the FA Cup final. A keen-tackling midfield player, he had just established himself in the Wednesday side when a series of niggling injuries hindered his progress. In seasons 1967–68 and 1968–69, he played in only eight games but bounced back the following season and when he left the club in May 1972 he had played in 156 games. His next club was Huddersfield Town and he later played for Chester, Barnsley and Scunthorpe United.

Q

QUICKEST GOAL. Charlie Tomlinson holds the club record for scoring the fastest goal in the league, when he netted after just 12 seconds in Wednesday's 1–0 win at Preston North End on 22 October 1949.

QUIGLEY, EDDIE. Eddie Quigley began his league career as a full-back with Bury but after scoring five goals as an emergency centre-forward at Millwall, he remained a forward. His movements were totally deceptive; his speed of thought and precise passing made him a constant threat to the opposition defences. He was capable of playing both inside- or centre-forward, though he preferred to play much deeper than most of his contemporaries. He joined Wednesday in October 1947 for a fee of £12,000. On Boxing Day 1947, he scored four goals as the Owls beat West Ham United 5–3 and then 24 hours later, he notched two goals in the return at Upton Park, which Wednesday won 4–1. He ended that season as the club's top scorer with 22 goals in 30 league appearances. He top scored again in 1948–49 and had scored ten goals in the first ten games of the following season when he was sold to Preston North End for a then British record fee of £26,500. He played for Blackburn Rovers before ending his playing career with Bury. Quigley went into management with non-league Mossley, later coaching Bury before managing Stockport County. In November 1966, he returned to Ewood Park as Jack Marshall's assistant, becoming manager on Marshall's resignation in February 1967. Despite exchanging duties with Johnny Carey to become chief scout, Quigley was sacked following the club's relegation to the third division. He found employment with Rovers a third time in 1979 under Howard Kendall, but when the now Sheffield United boss left in 1981, so did Quigley. Sadly, he died in April 1997.

QUINN, JOHN. St Helens-born John Quinn joined Wednesday from Prescot Cables in May 1959 and made his league debut four months later against Luton Town. However, over the next three seasons National Service and the form of Bobby Craig limited his opportunities and it wasn't until Alan Brown was appointed manager in 1964 that he was given an extended run in the first team. Though Quinn played many of his games at inside-forward, he filled a variety of positions in his later years at Hillsborough. A dedicated professional, he appeared in 195 games for the Owls, scoring 24 goals. In November 1967 he joined Rotherham United, playing in 114 league games for the Millmoor club before ending his league career at Halifax Town.

QUIXALL, ALBERT. A schoolboy international, Albert Quixall made his Wednesday debut with his future long-term wing partner Alan Finney against Chelsea at Hillsborough, scoring in a 2–2 draw. He was an important member of Wednesday's second division championship winning sides of 1951–52 and 1955–56 and was in outstanding form during the club's run to the FA Cup semi-finals in 1954. In 1956–57, he was the club's top scorer with 24 league and Cup goals, though it was often said that he never really reached his full potential whilst at Hillsborough. He represented the Football League and appeared for England Under-23s and the B side as well as winning the first of five full caps against Wales in 1953. In September 1958, Quixall moved to Manchester United for £45,000 – almost £10,000 more than the British record. He had scored 65 goals in 260 first team games, yet in his first season at Old Trafford, his goalscoring touch deserted him. He rediscovered it the following year and became a regular scorer, netting 56 goals in 183 appearances. He won an FA Cup winners' medal in 1963 but a year later signed for Oldham Athletic. In July 1966, he moved to Stockport County but retired after just one season at Edgeley Park.

R

RAPID SCORING. On Boxing Day 1911, Sheffield Wednesday beat Sunderland 8–0, with seven of their goals coming in the first half. Sam Kirkman, who was a great favourite with Wednesday supporters, opened the scoring in the third minute and added another after 20 minutes. Ted Glennon scored the fourth and sixth goals, whilst David McLean grabbed a first-half hat-trick. The Scotsman scored his fourth in the 58th minute before Wednesday took their foot off the accelerator. Five minutes from the end, Robertson, who had created four of Wednesday's goals, collided with Sunderland keeper Scott, leaving him completely dazed and unable to finish the match.

RECEIPTS. The club's record receipts are £533,918 for the FA Cup semi-final match between Sunderland and Norwich City on 5 April 1992. When Wednesday played Everton at Wembley in the FA Cup final of 1966, the receipts were £109,691. It was the first time receipts of over £100,000 had been taken.

RELEGATION. Sheffield Wednesday have been relegated on nine occasions. Their first taste came in 1898–99 when they lost 18 of their 34 matches, including a 9–0 beating at Derby County, but they were immediately promoted after just one season in the second division. They were next relegated in 1919–20 when they finished bottom of the first division with just 22 points. The club used no fewer than 41 players and won only seven matches. This time it took the Owls six seasons before they returned to the top flight but in 1936–37 they were relegated for a third time. After promotion in 1949–50, Wednesday lasted just one season in the first division before being relegated. The 1950s became known as the 'yo-yo years' as the club won promotion four times and were relegated on three occasions. Wednesday's seventh experience of relegation came in 1969–70, when they lost their last game of the season 2–1 at home to Manchester City. The club's worst-ever experience of relegation came in 1974–75 when for the first time in their history, the Owls were relegated to the third division after winning just five games. Wednesday's last experience of relegation came in 1989–90 when they finished third from the bottom of the first division, level on points with Luton Town but with a slightly inferior goal difference.

RICKETT, WALTER. Rickett began his football career with Sheffield United and scored with his first touch of the ball on his debut against Wednesday. He joined Blackpool and played in their 1948 FA Cup final side against Manchester United but after just 45 league appearances for the Blomfield Road club, he returned to Sheffield to join Wednesday in October 1949 for a fee of £6,000. Making his debut in a 1–0 win at Preston North End, he played in all the remaining 30 games that season to help Wednesday win promotion from the second division. Though the Owls were relegated the following season, Rickett was an important member of the side that won the second division championship in 1951–52. Surprisingly soon afterwards, he was sold to Rotherham United before ending his league career with Halifax Town.

RIMMER, ELLIS. Signed from Tranmere Rovers in February 1928, Ellis Rimmer arrived in time to help Wednesday escape from the threat of relegation to the second division, being on the losing side only once in his 15 appearances that season. He went on to help the Owls win two successive league championships, scoring his first hat-trick for the club in the first of those seasons, in a 4–2 win over Leeds United. His second hat-trick for Wednesday came in 1935–36, when he scored all three goals in a

141

3–3 draw with Everton, the club that had overlooked him in his younger days. On the tall side for a winger, Rimmer scored in every round of the club's famous FA Cup run of 1935 and then got two in the 4–2 win over West Bromwich Albion in the final. He was Wednesday's top scorer in 1934–35 with 26 goals from 44 appearances, a club record for a winger. He won four England caps, the first coming against Scotland at Wembley in 1930 when he scored two goals in a 5–2 win. In ten years with the club, he appeared in 418 league and Cup games and scored 140 goals before ending his career with Ipswich Town.

Ellis Rimmer

RITCHIE, JOHN. The most prolific goalscorer in Stoke City's history, John Ritchie took a particular liking to Sheffield Wednesday, hitting his first hat-trick against them in a 4–4 draw in 1963–64. The following season he scored all four goals in City's 4–1 win over the Owls. He became Wednesday's most expensive signing when he was allowed to leave the Victoria Ground for £70,000 in November 1966. He certainly began well enough at Hillsborough and hit a hat-trick in a 3–0 third-round FA Cup win over Queens Park Rangers. In his first two seasons with the Owls, he scored 37 goals in 77 games but in 1968–69 he suffered from injuries and at the end of the season he returned to Stoke for a meagre £25,000. During his time at Wednesday, he was called into the Football League side and scored twice in a 7–2 win over the League of Ireland. On his return to the Victoria Ground, he once again led the Stoke forward line with distinction, winning a League Cup winners' medal at Wembley in 1972.

ROBINSON, JACKIE. One of the greatest players in the club's history, Jackie Robinson was discovered by Billy Walker and given his debut at West Bromwich Albion in April 1935, where he scored Wednesday's goal in a 1–1 draw. It was midway through the 1936–37 season before he won a regular place in the Wednesday line up, yet within a few weeks, he was playing in an international trial. He made his international debut towards the end of that season, scoring one of England's goals in an 8–0 win over Finland in Helsinki. In 1938–39 when the Owls almost won promotion from the second division, he scored 19 league and Cup goals in 45 appearances. Just as he seemed to be reaching his peak, his league career was interrupted by the war years. Yet it was during the hostilities that Robinson produced some remarkable goalscoring feats. He scored 91 goals in 109 appearances, including six hat-tricks during the 1942–43 season. Despite scoring six goals in the first seven games

Jackie Robinson

of the 1946–47 season, he was allowed to join Sunderland for £7,500. It was then discovered that he was two years older than had been thought and the fee was reduced. Three years later he moved to Lincoln City, where a broken leg ended his career.

RODRIGUES, PETER. A former Welsh schoolboy and youth international, Peter Rodrigues was introduced to league football by his home-town club Cardiff City. In December 1965 after he had made 85 league appearances for the Ninian Park club, he signed for Leicester City for £45,000. In 1968–69, City were relegated to the second division, but also reached the FA Cup final, where they lost to Manchester City. Rodrigues, who by this time had been capped 23 times at full level by Wales, was wanted by a number of top-flight clubs but in October 1970 he joined second division Sheffield Wednesday for £50,000. At Hillsborough, Rodrigues took his tally of Welsh caps to 40 but he could not prevent Wednesday from slipping towards the third division and following relegation in 1974–75, he left to join Southampton. His career had a fairy-tale ending, as he captained the Saints to victory over Manchester United in the FA Cup final of 1976.

RUDDLESDIN, HERROD. Occasionally known as Harry, Ruddlesdin joined Wednesday in the summer of 1898 and made his debut in the second game of the following season as Nottingham Forest were defeated 2–1. Despite Wednesday, in their last season at Olive Grove, being relegated, Ruddlesdin did not miss a game following his debut and was one of the few players to come out of the season with any credit. In 1899–1900, Ruddlesdin was an ever-present as Wednesday won the second division championship. The following season, he again only missed one game – a model of consistency, he played in 94 consecutive league games from making his debut. He produced his best form in seasons 1902–03 and 1903–04 as Wednesday won and then retained the first division championship. This led to him making three appearances for England, the first against Wales in 1904. Towards the end of the 1905–06 season, he began to suffer from the illness which was to curtail his career and eventually cause his death at the early age of 33. He was only able to play in the club's FA Cup first-round win over Wolves as they went on to win the trophy against Everton in 1907 and would no doubt have appeared in many more than the 285 games he played in, had his life not been so tragically cut short.

RUMBLELOWS CUP. See Football League Cup.

RUNNERS-UP. Sheffield Wednesday have been runners-up in a division of the Football League on three occasions. In 1949–50, Wednesday finished runners-up to Tottenham Hotspur in the second division. After drawing 0–0 at home to the eventual champions, the Owls won promotion by 0.008 of a goal, beating both Sheffield United and Southampton who also finished with the same points total of 52. In 1960–61, Wednesday finished second to Tottenham Hotspur again, this time in the first division, but were eight points adrift of the brilliant London side, who also won the FA Cup. Spurs won their first 11 games with their first defeat coming in their 17th game of the season when Wednesday beat them 2–1 at Hillsborough with goals from Griffin and Fantham. In 1983–84, Wednesday ended the season as runners–up to Chelsea in the second division on goal difference – Chelsea's was +50, and the Owls' +38.

RUSSELL, DAVE. A former Dundee player, Dave Russell joined Wednesday in 1938 immediately after helping East Fife win the

Scottish Cup. Making his debut against Bury in the opening game of the 1938–39 season, he went on to play in every match of that campaign before his career with the Owls was interrupted by the war. A member of the successful British Army of the Rhine team, he also represented an All British XI against a Football League XI at Hillsborough in 1941. Joining the RAF, he was only able to appear in 62 wartime matches for Wednesday, but in 1942–43, he helped them to reach the League North War Cup final. After the war had ended, Russell took Denmark's national team to third place in the Olympic Games of 1948 and three years later became manager of Bury. After 11 seasons

Dave Russell

in charge at Gigg Lane, he joined Tranmere Rovers in a similar capacity before in 1969 becoming general manager, a position he relinquished in 1978.

S

SCANDAL. On 11 April 1964, the *People* newspaper carried a sensational story which claimed that Tony Kay, who had since joined Everton, Peter Swan and 'Bronco' Layne had accepted bribes to throw a match between Sheffield Wednesday and Ipswich Town in 1962. All three were immediately suspended and after appearing in court, were sent to prison and banned from playing football for life.

SCORES – HIGHEST. Wednesday's highest score in any league or Cup match is the 12–0 first-round FA Cup win over Halliwell on 17 January 1891. The club's best victory in the League Cup is 8–0 at Aldershot on 3 October 1989. The Owls also scored eight goals when beating Spora Luxembourg 8–1 in the UEFA Cup first-round first-leg tie at Hillsborough on 16 September 1992. In the Football League, Birmingham were beaten 9–1 on 13 December 1930 and Sunderland 8–0 on Boxing Day 1911.

SECOND DIVISION. Sheffield Wednesday have had nine spells in the second division. Relegated in 1898-99, the Owls won the second division championship in their first season out of the top flight and thus made an immediate return. The club won all of its 17 home matches and didn't lose a game until New Year's Eve. The club's second spell in division two lasted six seasons before they won the championship a second time in 1925–26, with Jimmy Trotter scoring 37 goals in 41 games. Wednesday's next spell in the second division also lasted six seasons, either side of the Second World War before promotion was won in 1949–50. Over the next nine years, Wednesday won the second division championship on three occasions: 1951–52, 1955–56 and 1958–59. On each occasion they spent only that one championship-winning season in division two. Relegated in 1969–70, the Owls had five seasons in the second division before dropping down to the third division for the first time in the club's history. Promoted in 1979–80, Wednesday played four seasons of second division football before promotion to the first division in 1983–84. Relegated in 1989–90, Wednesday finished third in the second division the following season and made yet again an immediate return to the top flight. Though Wednesday have had nine spells of second division football, five of them have been for one season only and in four of those, the club won the championship.

SEED, JIMMY. Jimmy Seed was working down the pits and playing for Whitburn in the Wearside League in his spare time when Sunderland offered him terms. At the outbreak of war he joined the Army. When he returned to Roker Park after the hostilities, he was turned away as the club felt it doubtful that he could fully recover from the effects of a slight gas attack suffered on active service. He joined Mid-Rhondda and after showing the gas had left no ill effects, was able to negotiate his own free transfer. In February 1920, he joined Spurs, soon settling in to become one of the club's most important and influential players of the decade. In 1921, he masterminded Spurs' FA Cup success and won the first of five England caps when he played against Belgium. He had played in 284 games for the White Hart Lane club, scoring 84 goals, when in August 1927 he was astonishingly allowed to move to Sheffield Wednesday, with 'Darkie' Lowdell joining Spurs in part-exchange. It must rank as the worst transfer decision ever made by Spurs. Towards the end of the 1927–28 season, the Owls were rock bottom of the first division, needing a desperate 16 points from ten games to stay up. Seed was made captain and inspired the Hillsborough club to pick up 17 points, four at the expense of Spurs who slumped miserably and were relegated.

Under Seed's guidance, Wednesday went on to win and retain the league title in the next two seasons. A member of the 1929 FA touring party to South Africa, Seed retired at the end of the 1930–31 season, having played in 146 games and scored 37 goals. At the invitation of Herbert Chapman, he moved into management with Clapton Orient before later taking charge at Charlton Athletic. Jimmy Trotter joined him at the Valley and they steered the club from the third division (south) to the first division in successive seasons from 1934 to 1936 before taking them to the FA Cup final in 1946 and 1947, winning the trophy on the second visit.

SEMI-FINALS. Up to the end of the 1996–97 season, Sheffield Wednesday had been involved in 14 FA Cup semi-finals and three League Cup semi-finals.

SEWELL, JACKIE. Beginning his career with Notts County, Jackie Sewell played alongside the legendary Tommy Lawton and in 179 league games scored 97 goals. In March 1951, Wednesday paid £34,500 – a British record – for his services. Though he scored six goals in ten appearances, he was unable to save the Owls from relegation to the second division. However, in 1951–52, he scored 23 goals as Wednesday won the division two title, including all four goals in a 4–2 win over Cardiff City. The first of six England caps came in November 1951 when Northern Ireland were beaten 2–0 at Villa Park. In 1954, he scored a hat-trick for the Football League against the League of Ireland at Maine Road. He scored a hat-trick in the opening game of the 1955–56 season as Wednesday beat Plymouth Argyle 5–2 but in December 1955 after scoring 92 goals in 175 games, he joined Aston Villa. At Villa Park, he won an FA Cup winners' medal in 1957 and scored 36 goals in 123 league appearances before ending his career with Hull City.

SHAW, JACK. Signed from Rotherham United in the summer of 1953, Jack Shaw had scored 134 league and Cup goals for the Millmoor side, including a club record 44 in the 1950–51 season. He made his Wednesday debut at Burnley in September 1953 and ended the season with 12 goals in 24 league matches. He had been bought to replace Derek Dooley but despite creating chances for

Sewell and Woodhead, he only managed 27 goals in his 65 games. His best moments came in the club's FA Cup run of 1950–51 when they reached the semi-final, Shaw scoring five goals in his eight appearances. He saw out his career with Wednesday in the reserves, playing most of his games at wing-half, though he was recalled to play in one more first-team game in 1957–58.

SHEFFIELD CHALLENGE CUP. The Sheffield Challenge Cup competition was a major event on the Sheffield football calendar and Wednesday were the first winners in 1877. Their successes were as follows:

1877 v Heeley	4–3 *aet*	
1878 v Attercliffe	2–0	
1881 v Ecclesfield	8–1	
1883 v Lockwood Brothers	2–1 after a 2–2 draw	
1887 v Collegiate	2–1	
1888 v Ecclesfield	3–2	

SHELTON, GARY. Given his first taste of league soccer with Walsall when only 16 years old, Gary Shelton moved to Aston Villa in January 1978 but in four seasons at Villa Park, he played in only 24 League games. Never getting the chance to establish himself with these two clubs, he jumped at the chance of joining Wednesday for £50,000 in March 1982. He not only made an immediate impact in the Wednesday midfield but scored some vital goals as the Owls won promotion to the first division in 1983–84. The following season, he

Gary Shelton

missed just one game in the top flight and was chosen as the over-age representative and captain of the England Under-21 side against Finland. In 1985–86 he suffered a number of minor injuries and loss of form but bounced back the following season to something like his old self. However, in the summer of 1987, he joined Oxford United, playing in 79 games for the Manor Ground club before moving to Bristol City. At Ashton Gate, Shelton helped the Robins win the third division championship in his first season with the club. He appeared in 180 games for City before joining Chester. Appointed player-coach at the Deva Stadium, he is still considered one of the best playmakers in the lower divisions.

SHERIDAN, JOHN. During his early years with Leeds United, John Sheridan had the misfortune to break his leg at Barnsley in October 1983 but recovered fully to be an ever-present the following season. A player with a great range of passing skills, his form didn't go unnoticed by Republic of Ireland manager Jack Charlton and in March 1988 Sheridan made his debut through parental qualification against Romania, winning the first of his 34 caps. After seven seasons at Elland Road in which he had played 267 first-team games, he joined Nottingham Forest for £650,000. Totally ignored at the City Ground, he played in just one League Cup match in three months before being rescued by Wednesday manager Ron Atkinson, who signed him for £500,000. Forming a midfield partnership with Carlton Palmer, he helped transform the Owls into an attractive passing side, only for them to lose five of their last six games and be relegated. He missed just one game the following season when the Owls won promotion at the first attempt. He will be forever remembered by Wednesday fans for the goal he scored against Manchester United in the 1991 League Cup final to bring the trophy to Hillsborough. Though hampered by injuries over the next few seasons, he had a hand in a couple of Wednesday's goals in the League and FA Cup finals of 1993 against Arsenal, but following the arrival of David Pleat in June 1995, he found himself out of favour. He had loan spells at Birmingham City and Bolton Wanderers before he joined the Trotters for £200,000 during the 1996–97 season.

SHINER, ROY. One of the few league players to hail from the Isle of Wight, Roy Shiner began his professional career with Huddersfield Town, but after just 21 league appearances in four seasons, he signed for Sheffield Wednesday. The Hillsborough club had just been relegated but in Shiner's first season, in which he was an ever-present, he scored 33 goals as Wednesday won the second division championship. He hit eight doubles and scored a hat-trick in the final game of the season when Lincoln City were beaten 5–3. In 1958–59 he won another second division championship medal, scoring 28 goals in 38 games, including a hat-trick in a 4–1 win at Scunthorpe United. In November of the following season, Shiner lost his place to Keith Ellis and joined Hull City. He had scored 96 goals in 160 league and Cup appearances for the Owls.

SHIRTLIFF, PETER. A brave central defender and the older brother of Paul, who played for Wednesday and Northampton Town between 1980 and 1985, he made his league debut for the Owls two months before turning professional in August 1978. He had just settled into the side when he lost out following the arrival of Mike Pickering from Southampton. He fought his way back and played an important part in helping Wednesday win promotion in 1983–84. However, with the emergence of Knight and competition from Hart, Madden and Smith, Shirtliff was once again out of favour and in the summer of 1986 he joined Charlton Athletic for £125,000. In his first season at The Valley, the club were involved in a play-off against second division Leeds United to see which team would play in the top flight the following season. Charlton were 1–0 down in extra-time with just seven minutes to go, when Shirtliff scored two late goals and saved the club from relegation. However, in July 1989, Ron Atkinson brought him back to Hillsborough for a then club record fee of £500,000. The Owls were relegated during his first season back but in 1990–91 he was a member of the side that won the League Cup and gained promotion. Injuries marred the next couple of seasons and in August 1993 he joined Wolverhampton Wanderers for £250,000. At the beginning of the 1995–96 season, he signed for Barnsley, playing a big part in the Oakwell club's revival. A popular player during his two spells at Hillsborough, he appeared in 359 first-team games.

SHUTT, CARL. Having been rejected by Wednesday, Carl Shutt finished up at Spalding United of the Northern Counties (East) League but in April 1985 after the Owls had given him another trial, he gave up his job to become a full-time professional. After coming on as a substitute in a 1–0 win at Oxford United in August 1985, he scored the equalising goal on his first full appearance as

Wednesday drew 2–2 at home to Coventry City. He scored nine goals in 17 games that season and was the hero of the club's fine FA Cup run, scoring both goals against Derby County, the winner against West Ham and the first goal of the semi-final, which Everton won 2–1 after extra-time. Despite scoring five times in the first ten matches of the 1986–87 season, he lost his place to David Hirst and was allowed to join Bristol City. His career at Ashton Gate was short-lived, though he did score all four goals in a 4–0 home victory over Fulham. In March 1989 he signed for Leeds United and though initially he found it difficult to make his mark, he won a second division championship medal in 1990 and a league championship medal in 1992. In the summer of 1993 he signed for Birmingham City but following a loan spell at Manchester City, he moved to Bradford City, where he scored the goal that took the Bantams into the play-offs and ultimately the first division.

SIMOD CUP. The Simod Cup replaced the Full Members' Cup in the 1987–88 season. Wednesday's first-round match that season saw them beat Bournemouth 2–0 at Hillsborough with Galvin and West the scorers. Drawn at home to Stoke City in round two, the Owls went down to the only goal of the game scored by George Berry. In 1988–89, the Owls reached the third round before going out to Queens Park Rangers.

SIMPSON, GEORGE. A firm favourite with the Wednesday fans, George Simpson joined the club from Jarrow in 1902 and made his debut in a goalless draw against Blackburn Rovers the following year. A skilful winger, he helped the club win the league championship in 1903–04 and the FA Cup in 1907. During the Owls' run to the final, he scored the only goal of the third-round replay win at Sunderland and headed the winning goal in the final at Crystal Palace as Wednesday beat Everton 2–1. The club from Roker Park were Wednesday's opponents when Simpson played his last game for the club in March 1909. The Owls went down 5–2 with Simpson scoring one of the goals. He had scored 39 goals in 160 league and Cup matches before signing for West Bromwich Albion along with Harry Burton.

SMALLEST PLAYER. Although such statistics are always unreliable for those playing before the turn of the century, it appears that the distinction of being Wednesday's smallest player goes to Harry Davis. In his day, he was without doubt the smallest player in the first division. Though he stood 5ft 4in, no player displayed more courage or tenacity than the little winger from Wombwell.

SMITH, MARK. Joining the Owls straight from school, Mark Smith made his debut at Colchester United towards the end of the 1977–78 season. By 1979–80, the season Wednesday won promotion from the third division, he was firmly established in the side and played in 44 league games, scoring 11 goals from the penalty spot. In each of the next three seasons, the dependable defender missed just one game and on each occasion, Wednesday failed to win. His consistent performances earned him six caps for England at Under–21 level, the first against the Republic of Ireland in 1981. He was an important member of the Wednesday side that won promotion to the first division in 1983–84 and an automatic choice in the club's first season back in the top flight. Yet the following season, he came under increasing pressure from Knight and Madden and in the summer of 1987 joined Plymouth Argyle, later playing for Barnsley and Notts County. He had loan spells with Chesterfield, Huddersfield and Port Vale before ending his career with Lincoln City.

SMITH, ROY. Signed from Selby Town in 1936, Roy Smith made his debut in a 1–0 defeat at Bolton Wanderers, replacing Jack Brown as the Owls' first-choice goalkeeper. Just when it seemed as if he was set for a good number of years, he was ousted by the good form of Derek Goodfellow who joined the club from Gateshead. He had just won his place back from Goodfellow when the war came. After the hostilities he was Wednesday's regular keeper for the 1946–47 campaign but the following season, after playing in 97 league and Cup games, he was allowed to join Notts County. He went on to make 110 league appearances for County but on his one and only return to Hillsborough, he conceded six goals, five of them scored by his former team-mate, Derek Dooley.

SMITH, WILF. Captain of Sheffield Boys and England Youth, German-born Wilf Smith made his Wednesday debut at wing-half in a 4–1 home win over Blackpool. He soon developed into a good full-back and when he appeared for the Owls in the FA Cup final of 1966, he was still only 19 years old. In 1967 he made the first of three appearances for the Football League and two years later represented the England Under-23s against Portugal. He made six appearances at this level and was unlucky not to win full honours. Following the Owls' relegation in 1969–70, he played in the opening game of the club's second division campaign of 1970–71 before joining Coventry City for £100,000. He had played in 233 first-team games, scoring five goals. He went on to appear in 135 league games for the Sky Blues before spells on loan with Brighton and Millwall and playing for Bristol Rovers and Chesterfield.

SNODIN, GLYN. A versatile performer, Rotherham-born Glyn Snodin began his career with Doncaster Rovers and in eight years at the Belle Vue club made 309 league appearances. He joined Sheffield Wednesday in June 1985 for a fee of £135,000 and made his debut in a disastrous 5–1 defeat at Tottenham Hotspur. At Hillsborough he settled into a left-sided defensive role, but despite some impressive performances, he was always in competition with Nigel Worthington. When the popular Irish international suffered an injury, Snodin became an automatic choice, though his temper often got the better of him. After being sent off, he missed the last few games of the 1986–87 season. He had made 73 first-team appearances when he joined Leeds United. In three years at Elland Road, he played in 94 league games, later playing for Oldham, Rochdale and Hearts.

SPIKSLEY, FRED. Fred Spiksley joined Wednesday by accident in January 1891. He was on his way from Gainsborough to sign for Accrington, when he was held up in Sheffield. He was met by John Holmes and Fred Thompson, who persuaded him to sign up for the Olive Grove side. He had the distinction of scoring the first hat-trick for Wednesday at Owlerton when he hit all three goals in the 3–2 first-round FA Cup defeat of Derby County on 21 January 1893. That year, he won the first of his seven England caps when he scored two goals in a 6–0 win over Wales at Stoke.

He followed this up with another brace in the 5–2 win against Scotland and one in the 2–2 draw with Ireland. He scored a number of vital goals for Wednesday, including two in the third-round FA Cup tie of 1893–94 against Aston Villa, as the Owls won 3–2 after being two goals down. In the FA Cup final of 1896, he scored both Wednesday's goals in the 2–1 win over Wolves and in 324 league and Cup appearances for the club, scored 116 goals. In his last representative game, he scored a hat-trick for the Football League against the Scottish League. After playing his last game for the club against West Bromwich Albion in April 1903 and scoring one of the goals in a 3–1 win, Spiksley left to play for Glossop, and later moved on to Leeds City and Southend before coaching abroad.

SPONSORS. The club's current sponsors are Sanderson Electronics Plc. Previous sponsors include MHS and Pinlux.

SPOORS, JIMMY. Discovered at Jarrow by Bob Brown, Wednesday's scout in the north east, Jimmy Spoors arrived at Hillsborough in April 1908 and made his league debut at centre-half in the 3–2 home win over Middlesbrough seven months later. When Willie Layton retired, Spoors moved to right-back and was virtually a permanent fixture there until halfway through the 1911–12 season when he switched to left-back to accommodate Worrall. The First World War interrupted his career and when peacetime football resumed in 1919, he played in a further 18 games, featuring at right-back, left-back and centre-half. He made the last of his 270 league and Cup appearances in the 2–0 home defeat by Bolton Wanderers in April 1920 before being given a free transfer and joining Barnsley.

SPRINGETT, PETER. Younger brother of Ron, he began his league career with Queens Park Rangers in 1963, making 139 first-team appearances before moving to Hillsborough in May 1967. It was a remarkable deal which saw brother Ron move back to Loftus Road for £16,000 whilst Wednesday paid £40,000 for Peter. In his first three years with the club, he missed only six of the first 112 league games before losing his place to Peter Grummitt whom manager Danny Williams bought from Nottingham Forest. He returned as first-choice keeper in 1973, playing in a total of 207 games for the club until the emergence of Peter Fox, when he retired to become a policeman.

SPRINGETT, RON. Joining Wednesday from Queens Park Rangers in March 1958, Ron Springett made his debut against Bolton Wanderers, keeping a clean sheet in a 1–0 win. Unfortunately, despite some heroic performances, he couldn't prevent Wednesday being relegated at the end of that season. However, he was a key member of the Owls side that won the second division championship the following season, keeping 13 clean sheets in the 32 matches in which he played. In 1959–60 he made the first of nine appearances for the Football League against the Irish League and won the first of 33 caps for England when he played against Luxembourg. In fact, Springett still holds the record of being Wednesday's most-capped England international. It was Springett's fine goalkeeping that kept the club in the upper reaches of the first division for six seasons in the early 1960s and yet, though he appeared in 384 games for Wednesday, he was never an ever-present. He won an FA Cup runners–up medal in 1966, but the following year returned to Loftus Road in a unique deal which brought his younger brother Peter to Hillsborough.

STANIFORTH, RON. One of the best full-backs in the game, Ron Staniforth began his league career with Stockport County before joining Huddersfield Town in May 1952. He helped the Leeds Road club to win promotion from the second division and reach a highest place of third in the first division. In 1954, he won eight full caps for England in the space of nine months. Staniforth arrived at Hillsborough in July 1955 and in his first season helped the club win the second division title, with one of his two goals being enough to beat Notts County. He had appeared in 107 first-team games for the Owls when he lost his place to Charlie Johnson and joined Barrow, first as player–manager and then as manager. He later had a spell at Hillsborough on the training staff before leaving the game for good.

STARLING, RONNIE. In Sheffield, Ronnie Starling, who died just before Christmas 1991, will be remembered not only as captain of the Wednesday team that won the FA Cup but also as the inspiration behind the Owls' dramatic 4–2 win over West

Bromwich Albion in 1935. By then, Starling was already an England international and at his third club. Born in the north east at Pelaw-on-Tyne near Gateshead on 11 October 1909, Starling went to work down the pit at Unsworth Colliery and then Washington Colliery in 1924. As an amateur, he attracted a lot of attention as a ball-playing inside-forward. The first to recognise his talents was Hull City boss Bill McCracken. For three seasons Starling learned his trade with the second division club and played a major part in their run to the semi-final of the FA Cup in 1929–30 when they took Arsenal to a replay. In May 1930,

Ronnie Starling

he joined Newcastle United for £4,000 but he was on the receiving end of some harsh treatment from the home fans and missed out on the Magpies' successful Cup run. A move to Sheffield Wednesday in the summer of 1932 was the start of his career taking off. Although he was signed by Bob Brown, it was his successor Billy Walker who got the best out of him. Walker recognised that players with Starling's gifts needed regular boosts to their confidence and in rebuilding Wednesday he made the inside-forward the captain and the focal point of the team. It paid off handsomely, for the Owls got to Wembley in 1935 and with Starling controlling the midfield, won 4–2. This Cup success came a couple of years after Starling had won international honours. After making 193 first-team appearances for the Hillsborough club, he was transferred to Aston Villa in January 1937 for £7,500, being seen as the man to lead the Midlands club out of division two. It was a shrewd choice for in 1938, Villa were second division champions and reached the semi-finals of the FA Cup. He remained at Villa throughout the war, retiring in 1948.

STEFANOVIC, DEJAN. Yugoslavian international Dejan Stefanovic was signed from Red Star Belgrade in December 1995 along with Darko Kovacevic. The elegant, left-sided defender made his Wednesday debut at Nottingham Forest on Boxing Day but struggled to adjust to the speed of the game as the Owls lost 1–0. Because of the club's desperate need for points, Stefanovic was not given many chances in 1995–96 but the following season, played in the majority of games and scored his first goal for the club in a 2–2 draw against Chelsea at Stamford Bridge.

STERLAND, MEL. Affectionately known as 'Zico' because of his tremendous ability at dead-ball situations, he originally started his career at Hillsborough as a midfielder but was converted to right-back in 1981–82. A series of niggling injuries prevented him from completing any season at Wednesday as an ever-present, though he did play in 39 matches when the Owls were promoted to the first division in 1983–84. Very dangerous with free-kicks around the edge of the box, he scored a number of great goals and in 1985–86 scored 11 league and Cup goals. His exciting displays eventually led to him being recognised by the international selectors and in November 1988 he won his only cap against Saudi Arabia. He would probably have remained at Sheffield Wednesday for the whole of his career but after inexplicably being relieved of the captaincy towards the end of 1988, he asked for a transfer and in March 1989 joined Rangers for £800,000. In his brief stay at Ibrox he helped Rangers to win the Scottish Championship, scoring three goals in nine appearances before moving to Leeds United at the end of the season. Reunited with Howard Wilkinson, he won a second division championship medal in 1989–90, was ever present for the first time in 1990–91 and in 1991–92 won a league championship medal. After missing the final stages of that championship-winning season through injury, he was forced to have a nine-month lay-off from the game. When he did return, he managed only five games before having to have a fourth operation on his ankle. Midway through the 1993–94 season, Leeds sadly terminated the contract of the former Owls favourite.

STEWART, JIMMY. Joining Wednesday from Gateshead NER, Jimmy Stewart made his debut for the Owls on St Valentine's Day 1903 in a 1–1 draw with Grimsby Town. By 1904–05, he had won a regular place in the Wednesday line up and had begun to show his goalscoring ability. He hit a hat-trick in a 4–0 win over Bury in January 1905, whilst the following season, he headed the club's goalscoring charts with 22 league and Cup goals. That season he scored another hat-trick in a 4–3 win at Nottingham Forest and four goals as Wolves were beaten 5–1 at Hillsborough. In 1906–07, his goals seemed to dry up but he did score an important goal in the FA Cup final as Wednesday beat Everton 2–1. That season Stewart made two appearances for England at full international level, scoring on his debut in a 1–1 draw against Wales at Fulham. He left Wednesday in 1908 to play for Newcastle United with whom he won a league championship medal; he played for them in the FA Cup final of 1911. Whilst with the Magpies he played for England against Scotland but later left St James's Park to end his career with Glasgow Rangers.

STRANGE, ALF. Alf Strange was working at a local colliery when a strike left him free to attend a trial with Portsmouth. The Fratton Park club had no hesitation in offering him terms and over the next couple of years, the free-scoring centre-forward enjoyed great success. However, in 1924 he was allowed to join Port Vale, where he played as an inside-forward. It was only when he signed for Sheffield Wednesday in 1927 that Strange began to make his name. Converted to wing-half, he formed part of the Strange-Leach-Marsden half-back line and during his time at Hillsborough, won 20 full caps for England. An ever-present in 1928–29 when the Owls won the League Championship, he missed only one game the following season, when the club won the title for the second year in succession. Towards the end of his career, he suffered from injuries and missed out on the club's FA Cup run of 1935. Later that year he joined Bradford, where he saw out his league career.

SWAN, PETER. Joining Wednesday as an amateur in May 1952, Peter Swan made his League debut in a 3–0 win at Barnsley in November 1955. Eventually he displaced Don McEvoy in the heart of the Wednesday defence and was an automatic choice in the side until his suspension in 1964. In 1958–59 he helped the Owls win the second division championship and won three caps for England at Under-23 level. In 1959–60, he was an ever-present as Wednesday finished fifth in the first division, and won the first of 19 full caps for England when he played in the 3–3 draw against Yugoslavia at Wembley. A key figure in the team that did so well in the early part of the 1960s, he was an ever-present again in 1962–63, but at the end of the following season, he was one of the Wednesday players banned from the game. In 1972, his life ban was lifted and he returned to Hillsborough hoping to make up for the eight years he had lost. In the event, he played in a further 15 games to bring his total number of first-team appearances for the club to 301 before moving to end his career with Bury.

SWIFT, HUGH. Beginning his career as an outside-left, Hugh Swift made his Wednesday debut during the Second World War in a match at Burnley in February 1942. When Ted Catlin was injured during the first leg of the 1943 League North War Cup final against Blackpool, Swift was moved to defence from where he never looked back. When league football resumed after the war, Swift formed an outstanding full-back partnership with Frank Westlake and in 1950 played for England B against Switzerland. On 11 February 1950, he suffered a double fracture of the jaw in Wednesday's 3–0 defeat at Coventry and did not play again for a couple of months, ending a run of 132 consecutive league appearances. Though he continued to play in 1950–51 he was still experiencing problems with his jaw and left the game following medical advice. Swift had appeared in 331 games for the Owls, including 136 in the war years.

SUBSTITUTES. The first-ever Sheffield Wednesday substitute was David Ford who came on for Don Megson against Sunderland at Hillsborough on 23 October 1965. The club had to wait until 6 May 1967 for their first goalscoring substitute – Jack Whitham scoring in the 7–0 home win over Burnley. The greatest number of substitutes used in a single season by Wednesday under the single substitute rule was 36 in 1975–76. Since 1986–87, two substitutes have been allowed and in 1991–92 75 were used. The greatest number of substitute appearances for Wednesday has been made by Trevor Francis, who came on during 47 league games with three more appearances in Cup-ties. Francis also holds the club record for the most individual appearances as a substitute in one season with 20 in seasons 1990–91 and 1991–92.

SUNDAY FOOTBALL. The first-ever Sunday matches in the Football League took place on 20 January 1974 as a result of the three-day week imposed by the government during its trial of strength with the coalminers. Wednesday's first league match on a Sunday was on 10 February when they beat Bristol City 3–1 in front of 15,888 spectators, with goals from Joicey, Henderson and Shaw.

SUSTAINED SCORING. During the 1951–52 season when Wednesday won the second division championship, the club discovered a new goalscoring sensation by the name of Derek Dooley. He didn't get into the side until 6 October, when he scored both goals in a 2–1 win over Barnsley. In the month of November, he scored 11 goals in four games, including five in the 6–0 win over Notts County. He also scored ten goals in the first four games in December, including all four as Everton were beaten 4–0 at Hillsborough. Scoring 22 goals in nine consecutive games, Dooley ended the season with 46 goals in 30 league games.

T

TALLEST PLAYER. It is impossible to say for definite who has been the tallest player ever on Sheffield Wednesday's books as such records are notoriously unreliable. One of the players certain to lay claim to the title is former Coventry City defender Andy Pearce who stood 6ft 4in. He appeared in 87 games for the Owls before joining Wimbledon for £700,000 in November 1995.

TAYLOR, ERIC. Spending almost 45 years at Hillsborough, Eric Taylor was the man behind the ambitious plans to make the ground into one of the best stadiums in the country. He joined Wednesday as an office boy in 1929 and five years later became assistant-secretary. In 1942 he became secretary–manager and for the next 16 years was in charge of team affairs, though he left the day-to-day coaching and training to his coaches – Bill Knox, Allan Brown and Jack Marshall. Under Taylor, Wednesday won promotion in 1949–50, 1951–52 and 1955–56 but were relegated in 1950–51 and 1957–58 – he dubbed these the 'yo-yo years'. After Wednesday's relegation in 1958, he relinquished team management responsibilities and concentrated on the administrative side of the club. He had never been afraid to enter the transfer market and in 1951 paid a British record £34,500 for Jackie Sewell. He also paid £12,000 for Eddie Quigley in 1947 and sold him for a record £26,500 in 1949. In the summer of

1967, he nearly died in a car crash. Never fully recovering he announced plans to retire in early 1974 but the following September he died.

TAYLOR, SAM. After playing his early football with Huddersfield Town either side of the First World War, Sam Taylor joined Wednesday in January 1921 and made his debut at Port Vale that month. An automatic choice for the next three seasons, he shared the top spot in the club's goalscoring chart of 1922–23 with 13 goals, including a hat-trick in a 4–1 win over Clapton Orient. He had scored 39 goals in 128 first-team appearances for the Owls when, after a dispute over terms, he left to join Southampton, later playing for Halifax, Chesterfield and Grantham Town.

TELEVISION. Sheffield Wednesday first appeared on BBC's *Match of the Day* on 9 January 1965 in a third-round FA Cup tie against Everton at Goodison Park. John Fantham and John Quinn scored for the Owls in a 2–2 draw. Wednesday lost the replay at Hillsborough four days later, 3–0.

THIRD DIVISION. Sheffield Wednesday were relegated to the third division for the only time in their history in 1974–75. Early into the following season, manager Steve Burtenshaw was dismissed and replaced by Len Ashurst but only a 2–1 victory in their final match against Southend United prevented the club from continuing the slide into the fourth division. In 1976–77, Ashurst took the club to eighth position, an increase of 12 places from the previous season but after ten games of the 1977–78 season, Wednesday were bottom of the League and it signalled the end of the road for the former Sunderland full-back. Jack Charlton was his replacement and after finishing 14th in both 1977–78 and 1978–79, the club finally gained their long-awaited promotion in 1979–80. It was an unbeaten run of 16 matches starting in mid-January that took the Owls to third place behind Grimsby Town and Blackburn Rovers. In 1979, the Sheffield Wednesday v Sheffield United match attended by 49,309 broke the record for the highest attendance at a third division match.

THOMPSON, GARRY. Birmingham-born Garry Thompson began his league career with Coventry City, where he scored 38 goals in 134 appearances and made his debut for the England Under-21 side. In February 1983 he joined West Bromwich Albion and scored 39 goals in 91 games before signing for Sheffield Wednesday for what was then a club record fee of £450,000. He failed to adapt his style of play to fit in with Wednesday's pattern and though he scored in four consecutive games around the turn of the year, he left the club after just one season to join Aston Villa. He later played for Watford, Crystal Palace, Queens Park Rangers and Cardiff City before joining Northampton Town in 1995.

THOMPSON, JACK. Signed from Blyth Spartans in the summer of 1933, Jack Thompson made his debut for Wednesday at the age of 18 in a first division match against Sunderland in November of that year. A talented inside-forward, his early years at Hillsborough were hampered by injuries and then when he had recovered, he faced stiff opposition from Robinson, Starling and Napier to name but three. He had appeared in 36 first-team games when the Second World War broke out and went on to score 51 goals in 111 wartime matches for the club. In 1946 he signed for Doncaster Rovers, playing in 59 league matches for the Belle Vue club before ending his career with Chesterfield, for whom he turned out on 82 occasions.

TOMLINSON, CHARLIE. After joining the Hillsborough groundstaff straight from school, Charlie Tomlinson was allowed to leave the club four years later in 1939 after manager Jimmy McMullan felt he would struggle to make the grade. Tomlinson joined Bradford but within weeks war broke out and he was restricted to guesting for Rotherham before netting 25 goals in 90 wartime games for Wednesday. When football resumed after the hostilities, he continued to play for Wednesday after Eric Taylor had paid Bradford £1,000 for his services and in 1945–46 he scored a hat-trick in a 6–1 FA Cup win against York City at Bootham Crescent. He turned in some outstanding performances for the Owls and in October 1949 scored the quickest goal in the club's history, netting after 12 seconds of the match against Preston North End. He played in 77 league and Cup games before joining Rotherham United in March 1951.

TRANSFERS. Sheffield Wednesday's current record transfer fee paid is £2.75 million, a figure they paid for both Des Walker from Sampdoria and Andy Sinton from Queens Park Rangers, both in August 1993. The club's record fee received is the £2.75 million they got for Paul Warhurst when he joined Blackburn Rovers, also in August 1993. However, some unusual arrangements have been made in the transfer of Wednesday players. When Tom Brandon was with Blackburn Rovers, Wednesday promised him a public house if he would join the club. Rovers complained to the Football League and Wednesday were blacklisted for a time. Alec Brady and Jack Madden of Celtic were both signed by Wednesday after playing in a practice match. It then transpired that a Roman Catholic priest had followed the two players from Glasgow to persuade them to go back and so both were sent into hiding. Unfortunately, Madden was discovered by the priest and taken back to Scotland, but Brady remained with Wednesday and scored the club's first hat-trick in the Football League. Billy Felton was with the Grimsby Town side travelling to Accrington for a third division (north) match when he was asked to leave the train at Sheffield to sign for the Owls which he did. That afternoon he made his Wednesday debut against Southampton at Hillsborough. His full-back partner Ernest Blenkinsop joined the Owls from Hull City, who it is rumoured signed him from Brierley Colliery for £100 and 80 pints of beer. Jackie Sewell was accorded the title of 'worth his weight in gold' when he was transferred from Notts County to Sheffield Wednesday for £34,500. At the time, the price of gold was fixed at $35 an ounce, so the comparison was more meaningful than it would be today. Since then, the price of players has inflated to least twice the rate of the price of gold.

TROTTER, JIMMY. Beginning his league career with Bury, Jimmy Trotter scored 29 goals in 40 games for the Gigg Lane club before joining Wednesday for £2,500 in February 1922. He made his debut for the Owls against Wolverhampton Wanderers, scoring the opening goal in a 3–1 win. However, despite this impressive start, he suffered from a shoulder injury and did not win a regular place in the Wednesday side until October 1924. Replacing Sid Binks, Trotter hit all five goals in Wednesday's 5–2 victory over Portsmouth in December 1924 and repeated the feat in September 1925 when Stockport County were beaten 6–2. In that 1925–26 season, Trotter scored 37 goals to help the club win promotion from the second division and in 1926–27 he scored another 37 league goals to top the first division goalscoring charts. These goalscoring feats remained club records until Derek Dooley's achievement in 1951–52. Trotter was a prolific goalscorer and in 160 first-team appearances, scored 114 goals, including seven hat-tricks. His career with Wednesday was curtailed due to injuries and the emergence of Jack Allen, and in 1929 he joined Torquay United. He later played for Watford before becoming Jimmy Seed's assistant at Charlton Athletic. His final years in the game were spent as Charlton's manager after having had a spell as England's trainer when Walter Winterbottom was manager.

TURNER, CHRIS. One of the most popular goalkeepers to have played for the club, Chris Turner made his debut for Wednesday in a goalless draw at home to Walsall on the opening day of the 1976–77 season. In fact that season the young keeper was in such good form that he played in five games for the England Youth team. Turner kept 15 clean sheets in his first season including four games in succession but, in the summer of 1979, he was allowed to leave Hillsborough and joined Sunderland for £90,000. He played in 195 league games for the Roker Park club before signing for Manchester United for what was then a club record fee for a goalkeeper of £250,000. Despite competition from Gary Bailey, he played in 79 games but left the club in 1988 to return to Sheffield Wednesday. He took his tally of league games for the club to 166 before joining Leyton Orient after a loan spell at Leeds United.

TWINS. The only instance of twins playing in Wednesday's league side was when former Dukinfield players Derek and Eric Wilkinson played together in the 3–3 draw against Sunderland at Roker Park on 10 September 1958.

U

UEFA CUP. After finishing third in the first division in 1991–92, Sheffield Wednesday entered the following season's UEFA Cup competition full of confidence. An emphatic first-round defeat of Spora Luxembourg (home 8–1, away 2–1) – in which Paul Warhurst swallowed his tongue and collected three goals, as an early indication of his goalscoring potential, preferred great optimism for the club's second-round tie against Kaiserslautern of Germany. In a bad-tempered affair in Germany, Wednesday's David Hirst was sent-off in a 3–1 defeat for the Yorkshire side, after he had given them the lead. Goals from Danny Wilson and John Sheridan in a 2–2 draw at Hillsborough went some way towards making amends but the Owls were out of the competition.

UNDEFEATED. Sheffield Wednesday have remained undefeated at home throughout four league seasons: 1899–1900, 1903–04, 1928–29 and 1934–35. The club's best and longest undefeated home sequence in the Football League is 31 matches between 13 December 1902 and 29 October 1904. Wednesday's longest run of undefeated league matches home and away is 19 between 3 December 1960 and 17 April 1961.

UTILITY PLAYERS. A utility player is one of those particularly gifted footballers who can play in several or even many different

167

positions. Three of Sheffield Wednesday's earliest utility players were Albert Mumford, Tom Brittleton and Bill Hemmingfield. Albert Mumford played in every position on the field, including goalkeeper in the match against Sunderland Albion when he was only beaten by a penalty. Tom Brittleton arrived at Hillsborough as an inside-forward but after playing at full-back, centre-half and centre-forward, eventually settled down at wing-half, going on to make 373 appearances for the Owls. Hemmingfield gave fine service to Wednesday and though he played in only 47 first-team games, he filled seven different positions. Johnny Quinn who played in 195 games for Wednesday between 1959 and 1967, wore eight different numbered outfield shirts. After the mid-1960s, players were encouraged to become much more adaptable and to see their role as less stereotyped. At the same time, much less attention came to be paid to the implication of wearing a certain numbered shirt and accordingly some of the more versatile players came to wear almost all the different numbered shirts at some stage or another, although this did not necessarily indicate a vast variety of positions. Chris Bart-Williams has been talented enough to wear seven different numbered shirts in his 152 league and Cup games for Wednesday.

V

VARADI, IMRE. A fast, tricky forward, Imre Varadi was born in London of Hungarian parents. An acknowledged goalscorer, his career appeared to be in tatters in 1978, when non-league Letchworth Town asked him to leave. He was spotted playing in Sunday league football by Sheffield United manager Harry Haslam and offered terms. He had played only ten league games for the Blades when Everton paid £80,000 for him. Two years later, he looked set to join Benfica but the deal fell through at the last moment. After becoming a free agent in 1981 he moved to Newcastle United for £125,000. Then came the chance to return to Sheffield, with Wednesday paying £150,000 for his services in August 1983. He ended his first season at Hillsborough as the club's top scorer and again in 1984–85 when he hit a hat-trick in a 5–0 win over Leicester City. After rejecting terms, he moved to West Bromwich Albion and later Manchester City before returning to Hillsborough for a second spell in September 1988. He had scored three goals in 22 league games before signing for Leeds United in February 1990. In both spells, Varadi played in 120 first-team games, scoring 46 goals. After loan spells at Luton and Oxford, he joined Rotherham United on a free transfer. He later played for Mansfield and Scunthorpe before becoming player–manager of Matlock Town.

Imre Varadi

VICTORIES IN A SEASON – HIGHEST. In the 1958–59 season, Sheffield Wednesday won 28 of their 42 League fixtures to win the second division championship, the highest number of wins in a season in the club's history. In 1925–26, they won 27 of their 42 division two matches to win the championship with 60 points.

VICTORIES IN A SEASON – LOWEST. Wednesday's poorest performance was in 1974–75 when they won only five matches out of their 42 league games and finished bottom of the second division.

VIDEOS. Sheffield Wednesday have produced a number of videos in conjunction with the BBC, the most notable being an official history of the club.

W

WADDLE, CHRIS. One of the most exciting players ever to play for Sheffield Wednesday, Chris Waddle began his league career with Newcastle United, who signed him from Tow Law Town. He made his debut for the Magpies in October 1980 and the following season was an ever-present. In 1983–84 he was part of the Newcastle side that won promotion to the first division and remained a regular member of the squad for the next six seasons. But in the summer of 1985, after scoring 52 goals in 190 first-team appearances, he was sold to Tottenham Hotspur for £590,000, following a well-publicised dispute with Magpies manager Jack Charlton. He had an excellent second season at White Hart Lane, playing in 39 games as Spurs reached the FA Cup final, only to lose to Coventry City, and finished third in the first division. Plagued by injury and loss of form, he had a disastrous 1987–88 but came back strongly in the next campaign in a

Chris Waddle

new creative midfield role, to be ever present and top scorer. With Spurs facing great financial problems, he was sold to French League champions, Marseilles for £4.25 million, a new record fee for an English player. In three seasons with the French club, he won three league championship honours and reached the 1991 European Cup Final. Marseilles lost on penalties to Red Star Belgrade. He joined Sheffield Wednesday in the summer of 1992 for £1 million and despite having played the last of his 62 England internationals against Turkey in October 1991, he was voted the Football Writers' Association Player of the Year in 1992–93. The club finished sixth in the League and were runners-up in both the League and FA Cup finals. In 1996–97 Waddle joined Bradford City after Owls' fans had earlier wanted him to be given the assistant-manager's job. He ended the season with Sunderland but failed to prevent the Wearside club from losing their premiership status. Now player–manager of Burnley, he is a wonderfully gifted player. Chris Waddle will always be remembered at Hillsborough for the many magic moments he provided.

WALKER, BILLY. The son of former Wolves full-back George Walker, Billy Walker first played for Hednesford Town and Darlaston and was playing for Wednesbury Old Athletic when Aston Villa signed him on amateur forms in 1915. A free-scoring inside-forward, he turned professional in 1919 and scored both goals on his Villa debut in a 2–1 FA Cup win over Queens Park Rangers. He scored three more goals that season as Villa went on to win the Cup. The following season he scored 27 league goals and won the first of his 18 England caps. One of the greatest players ever to pull on a Villa shirt, he played in 531 league and Cup games, scoring 244 goals and was the first player to score a hat-trick of penalties in a league game. In December 1933 he was appointed manager of Sheffield Wednesday. When he arrived at Hillsborough, the Owls were struggling near the foot of the First Division but under Walker's managership, they embarked on a 12 match unbeaten run, finishing the season in mid-table. He soon found some success, for in 1935 he took the Owls to the FA Cup final, where they beat West Bromwich Albion 4–2 at Wembley. They narrowly escaped relegation the following season but in 1936-37 they went down to the second division. After just 14 games of the 1937–38 campaign, the Owls were second from the bottom in division two and Walker resigned after a rather stormy meeting of shareholders. After a break from football he took over as manager of non-league Chelmsford City but in March 1939, he began a long association with Nottingham Forest, where he remained as manager until ill-health forced him to resign in 1960. During his reign at the City Ground he led Forest to the third division championship in 1950–51, promotion to the first division in 1956–57 and victory in the FA Cup final in 1959.

WALKER, DES. One of England's most effective central defenders, Des Walker made his league debut for Nottingham Forest in March 1984 but had to wait until 1985–86 before establishing himself in the Forest side. By 1987–88 he was being described by a number of judges as the best central defender in the country, yet he wasn't called up by England manager Bobby Robson until the following season. He then became an automatic choice. He has won 59 caps for his country, and was voted the outstanding player in the 1990 World Cup tournament. At Forest he helped the club to a series of great League and FA Cup runs, but at the end of his contract in 1992, he exercised his option to move and signed for Italian club Sampdoria for £1.5 million, a pre-determined fee which was well below his true market value. Never settling on the Continent, his Italian nightmare was brought to an end when Trevor Francis signed him for Sheffield Wednesday for £2.7 million in July 1993. Still noted for his terrific recovery rate, Walker is one of the most outstanding sweepers of the post-war era. Cool under pressure, he continues to perform brilliantly for a Wednesday side whose supporters readily acknowledge his contribution to the club's improved performances.

WALKER, TOMMY. Right-back Tommy Walker began his league career with Bradford City before joining Sheffield Wednesday for £1,900 in February 1926. Making his debut at home to Hull City he helped steady the side in Wednesday's run-in to the second division championship. Forming a solid full-back partnership with Ernest Blenkinsop, Walker won league championship medals in 1928–29 and 1929–30. Though he missed very few games over ten seasons at Hillsborough, he was surprisingly left out of the side during Wednesday's run to the 1935 FA Cup final. He did, though, receive a medal. He played his last game for the

Owls at West Bromwich Albion in April 1935 before joining the club's training staff. He stayed with the club until 1967 when Wednesday manager Alan Brown decided to make changes in the club's backroom staff.

WARHURST, PAUL. After four months at Maine Road in which he wasn't given a chance to prove himself, Paul Warhurst was surprisingly transferred to Oldham Athletic. He established himself in the side at central defence during the club's historic double Cup runs, but in 1990–91 he was switched to right-back with great success and became a regular member of the England Under-21 side. In the summer of 1991 he was sold to Sheffield Wednesday for £750,000 and after a mixed first season, he was asked by Trevor Francis to play as a striker as the club had major injury problems. Reluctantly he agreed but astounded everyone by scoring six in the League and 12 in Cup competitions. In January and February 1993, he equalled Derek Dooley's post-war record of scoring in seven successive games for the club. In August 1993 Warhurst joined Blackburn Rovers for £2.7 million but was struck down by a succession of injuries and illnesses, including breaking both legs within a year.

WARTIME FOOTBALL. In spite of the outbreak of war in 1914, the major football leagues embarked upon their planned programme of matches for the ensuing season and these were completed on schedule at the end of April the following year. Wednesday finished seventh in the first division, David McLean top-scoring with 22 goals in 33 games, including hat-tricks in a 5–2 win over Aston Villa and a 6–0 thrashing of Bradford. Wednesday decided to enter re-arranged wartime football in time for the 1915–16 season and though they finished seventh in the Midland Section (Principal Tournament), it was a poor substitute for a club which, before the outbreak of war, had been one of the top sides in the country. During the 1916–17 campaign, Wednesday's Tom Cawley was loaned to Bradford because when they arrived at Hillsborough they were a man short. Cawley scored two goals for the visitors in a 3–1 win! When Bradford City visited Hillsborough later in the season, Brelsford of Wednesday and City's Torrance were sent off and though the match was immediately abandoned with five minutes still to play,

Paul Warhurst

the result, a 1–0 win for the Owls, was allowed to stand. Ted Glennon who scored 54 goals in 117 wartime appearances netted four in a 5–0 win over Sheffield United at Bramall Lane on 16 March 1928. In contrast to the events of 1914, once war was declared on 3 September 1939, the football league programme of 1939–40 was immediately suspended and the government forbade any major sporting events, so that for a short while there was no football of any description. Wednesday had opened the season with a 3–0 reversal at Luton Town, following it with a 3–1 win at home to Barnsley. Charlie Napier scored two of the goals. On 2 September they lost 1–0 at Hillsborough against Plymouth Argyle and when war broke out, they were near the foot of the second division. After spending the first season of wartime football in the East Midlands Regional Division, the Owls joined the North Regional League which was decided on goal average alone and points were not awarded. It was a disastrous season for Wednesday as they finished 34th out of 36 clubs. The only incident of note occurred on Christmas Day 1940, when the match at Sheffield United was played at Hillsborough owing to Blitz damage at Bramall Lane. The war also ended Jimmy McMullan's management career, for in 1942 his contract was not renewed by the Wednesday board. Eric Taylor, who began his time at Hillsborough as an office boy in 1929 was appointed secretary–manager. In his first season in charge, he helped the Owls to reach the League North War Cup final, which they lost 4–3 over two legs to Blackpool. Hillsborough was the venue for a number of representative games including a Football League XI v All British XI in 1941 and an England v Scotland Army international in 1942, thus ensuring extra income was generated.

WESTLAKE, FRANK. Full-back Frank Westlake made his league debut for Wednesday in a 2–2 draw at Luton Town in March 1938. However, because he was not registered, he was banned for the rest of that season and Wednesday were fined. During the war years, he played in 35 games for the Owls before becoming a first-team regular in 1946. He partnered Hugh Swift at full-back, the two of them appearing in 103 consecutive games. After losing his place to Vic Kenny he left Wednesday to play for Halifax Town.

WHARNCLIFFE CHARITY CUP. Wednesday were the first

winners of the Wharncliffe Charity Cup when they beat Heeley 3–2 in 1879. The club's successes were as follows:

1879 v Heeley   3–2
1882 v Heeley   5–0
1883 v Pye Bank   4–0
1886 v Heeley   2–0
1888 v Rotherham   2–0

Wednesday lost to Heeley in the finals of 1880 and 1885 and were beaten by Staveley in the final of 1887.

WHITHAM, JACK. After being turned down by his home-town club Burnley, Jack Whitham joined Sheffield Wednesday in November 1964. It was therefore fitting that when he did make his first-team debut for the Owls on 6 May 1967, their opponents were Burnley. Whitham came on as a substitute for Brian Usher and scored two goals in a 7–0 rout of the Turf Moor club. Though he possessed the instincts of a natural goalscorer, he was seldom able to shake off injuries and enjoy a long run in the side. However, the blond striker is ensured of a lasting place in the club's history for his hat-trick in one of the most unforgettable matches ever played at Hillsborough. The Owls entertained the European Cup holders Manchester United and beat them 5–4 in front of a 51,931 crowd. In fact, there were many who credited Whitham with four goals that day, as he was the nearest to Nobby Stiles when the United player headed into his own net. He had scored 31 goals in 71 appearances when he was surprisingly sold to Liverpool for £57,000 in May 1970. He appeared in only 16 games for the Anfield club yet scored a powerfully struck hat-trick against Derby County before moving to Cardiff City and later ending his career with Reading.

WHITTINGHAM, GUY. Evesham-born Guy Whittingham joined Portsmouth from Yeovil Town in June 1989 on a free transfer. Immediately settling into the Fratton Park side, he top-scored in his first season with 23 goals. A prolific goalscorer throughout his four seasons at Pompey, he had scored 104 goals in 188 games when he signed for Aston Villa for £1.2 million in the summer of 1993. He had hardly established himself at Villa Park when he was loaned out to Wolverhampton Wanderers before joining Sheffield Wednesday for £700,000 in December

1994. He made his debut against Everton at Goodison Park on Boxing Day, scoring twice in a 4–1 win. Two days later he hit another brace in a 5–1 beating of Coventry City. A well-respected striker, he has now moved into midfield from where he still continues to score goals.

WILKINSON, DEREK. Joining Wednesday from Cheshire League side Dukinfield in November 1953, Derek Wilkinson was primarily a winger who could play on either flank, although he did make a number of appearances at both inside- and centre-forward. Though he played in a handful of matches after making his debut at Cardiff City in November 1954, he had to wait until the 1957–58 season before establishing himself in the Wednesday side. He was an important member of the side that won the second division championship in 1958–59, scoring 12 goals in 39 appearances. In the 3–3 draw at Sunderland during that season, he and his twin brother Eric appeared together. It remains the only time that twins have played in the same match for Wednesday's first team. Not a prolific goalscorer, 57 in his 223 league and Cup games, Derek scored both Wednesday's goals in a 2–0 sixth-round FA Cup win over Sheffield United at Bramall Lane in March 1960. He gave the club great service until 1965 when injury forced him to leave the game.

WILKINSON, HOWARD. After joining Sheffield Wednesday as a professional in the summer of 1962, winger Howard Wilkinson found his first-team opportunities limited and in July 1966 after appearing in 22 games, he moved to Brighton and Hove Albion. At the Goldstone Ground he played in 129 league games, scoring 19 goals. Wilkinson started his managerial career at non-league Boston United and gained a Physical Education degree at Sheffield University. After teaching for a while, he became an

Howard Wilkinson

FA regional coach and managed England's semi-professional international team. In July 1982, he was appointed manager of Notts County but spent only one season in charge at Meadow Lane before taking over at Hillsborough. During his spell at County he became England's Under-21 coach and later manager. In his first season in charge, he took the Owls back into the first division and despite having little money to spend on strengthening the squad, he took them to the 1985–86 FA Cup semi-finals and fifth place in the top flight. He left Hillsborough in October 1988 to join Leeds United whom he took to the second division championship in 1989–90. After finishing fourth in the first division the following season, Leeds won the league championship in 1991–92, pipping Manchester United in an exciting run-in.

WILKINSON, JACK. After scoring over 100 goals for Dearne Valley Old Boys, Jack Wilkinson joined Wath Athletic before signing for Wednesday in October 1925. He made his debut as an 18-year-old outside-left, scoring one of the goals in a 2–0 win over Hull City. He played in the last seven games of the 1925–26 season, scoring three goals as the Owls won six of the matches to gain promotion to the first division as champions of division two. Over the next two seasons, he was a regular member of the Wednesday side but lost his place to Ellis Rimmer towards the end of the 1927–28 season. After that, he played in only a handful of matches before leaving Hillsborough to sign for Newcastle United. Though he suffered from cartilage trouble, he went on to play for Lincoln, Sunderland and Hull before ending his career with non-league Scunthorpe United.

WILLIAMS, DANNY. After starting his career as an inside-forward, Danny Williams made his name as a wing-half for Rotherham United, making 459 League appearances for the Millmoor club. In 1962 he took over as manager but quit three years later, intending to retire from football and run his sports outfitter's shop in the town. Within a couple of months, however, he had joined Swindon Town. He had great success at the County Ground, taking the club to promotion to division two and to a League Cup final victory over Arsenal in 1969 when they were still a third division club. Appointed manager of Wednesday in

July 1969, his spell in charge was disastrous. The Owls were a club in decline and in his first season they were relegated to the second division. They were struggling at the foot of division two when he was sacked in January 1971. Towards the end of the year he was back in football as manager of Mansfield Town but after the Stags suffered relegation in 1971–72, he moved back to Swindon Town for a second spell in charge. Again he experienced relegation in 1973–74 and though they came close to making an immediate return, he later retired to South Yorkshire.

WILLIAMS, REES. Although only 5ft 5ins, right-winger Rees Williams turned in some outstanding displays for Wednesday following his transfer from Merthyr Town in the summer of 1922. He made his debut in the opening game of the 1922–23 season in a 2–1 win at Rotherham and went on to become a regular member of the side for the next five seasons. He played in 173 league and Cup games for the Owls and though he scored only eight goals, he created many more for his team-mates. He was capped four times by Wales during his stay at Hillsborough, winning his first cap against Scotland in 1923. Following the arrival of Mark Hooper from Darlington, Williams lost his place and in October 1927, he joined Manchester United, playing in 35 games for the Old Trafford club.

WILSON, ANDREW. Arriving at Wednesday from Clyde in 1900, Andrew Wilson took a little time to settle, but even so, he ended his first season at the club as the leading scorer with 13 goals. In a career that spanned 20 years, Wilson was leading scorer in eight of his 16 seasons, scoring 216 goals in 545 league and Cup games. Yet for all that, he only scored two hat-tricks, against Everton (home 4–1) in 1902–03 and Woolwich Arsenal (home 6–2) in 1908–09. He won league championship medals in 1902–03 and 1903–04 and scored twice in the FA Cup semi-final of 1907 as Woolwich Arsenal were beaten 3–1 and then set up Simpson's winning goal in the final itself. Wilson won six full caps for Scotland, the first coming against England in 1907 and the last seven years later against Ireland, but there were many who felt he should have had more. During the First World War, he appeared in a further 75 games for Wednesday, scoring 25 goals. When league football resumed in 1919–20, he played in just one more game, at Liverpool, before retiring to concentrate on a career in management, which took him to Bristol Rovers, Oldham Athletic and Stockport County.

WILSON, CHARLES. Despite playing for Sheffield Boys, Yorkshire Boys and England Boys, Charles Wilson was overlooked by both local clubs and began his league career with West Bromwich Albion. He scored 42 goals in 123 league appearances for the Hawthorns club before signing for Wednesday in February 1928. Making his debut at home to Newcastle United, he played in just five games that term, scoring two goals in the 5–0 thrashing of Burnley. However, he failed to establish himself as a forward and played at full-back before having his longest run in the side at left-half in 1930–31 when the Owls finished third in the first division. The following season he played only in three games – all victories – before losing out to Smith and in March 1932 he joined Grimsby Town, later playing for Aston Villa.

WILSON, GEORGE. Despite joining Blackpool as a centre-forward, it was as a centre-half that George Wilson made his name. He left Bloomfield Road in March 1920 for a fee of £3,000 after eight years with the Seasiders. He made his debut for the Owls in a 2–2 home draw with Liverpool and though he impressed in the last few months of the season, he could not prevent Wednesday being relegated to the second division. Appointed club captain, he won 12 full England caps between 1921 and 1924, making his international debut in a goalless draw with Wales at Cardiff. Wilson also captained his country on three occasions, the last being in 1923 when Sheffield United's Billy Gillespie captained the Irish. He appeared in 197 league and Cup games for Wednesday, leaving the club to join third division (north) club, Nelson, just prior to the Owls' promotion-winning season of 1925–26.

WINTERBOTTOM, HARRY. Though on the small side, winger Harry Winterbottom was reported to be one of the best and fastest players of his day. His early clubs included Suffolk, Alexandria, Talbot Street, Heeley, Exchange, Providence and Lockwoods before he joined Wednesday. Though the club turned professional in 1887, Winterbottom, who worked as a bone haft and scale cutter, a very skilful job, was happy to continue as an amateur. He was an important member of the Wednesday side that reached its first FA Cup final in 1890. He played in every game during the run to the final, scoring the winning goal against Accrington but unfortunately he was injured and missed Wednesday's 6–1 beating by Blackburn Rovers at the Kennington Oval.

WITCOMB, DOUG. Signed from West Bromwich Albion for £6,000 towards the end of the 1946–47 season, the twice-capped Welsh international played in one more match, against Northern Ireland, whilst with Wednesday. He made his debut for the club in the 5–1 defeat of Spurs and helped Wednesday avoid relegation to the third division. An important member of the side that won promotion in 1949–50, he missed just one match that season and two the following one when they went straight back down. In 1951–52, he suffered a bad injury and was forced to miss the middle part of the season but returned just in time to see the Owls clinch the second division title. The arrival of George Davis from Oswestry meant Witcomb lost his place and after making 230 first-team appearances, he joined Newport County, where he played in 25 league games for the Somerton Park club.

WOODHEAD, DENNIS. The grandson of Billy Betts, Dennis Woodhead made his Wednesday debut at home to Newcastle United in May 1947. During his nine seasons with the club, he helped them to win promotion in 1949–50 and 1951–52, though his best season was 1953–54. During that season, the left-winger, who could also play centre-forward, scored 21 goals in 45 games, ending the campaign as the club's top goalscorer. He played the last of his 226 games for Wednesday at home to Everton in March 1955, a relegation season for the Owls. In September 1955 he joined Chesterfield, later having an excellent short spell with Derby County for whom he scored 24 goals in 94 league appearances. Woodhead returned to Hillsborough in the summer of 1971 when he replaced Derek Dooley as the club's commercial manager, a post he held until 1987.

WOODS, CHRIS. Chris Woods sprang to fame in 1977–78 when he played in every match from the third round to the final of the League Cup with Nottingham Forest, and kept two clean sheets, as the City Ground club won 1–0 after a 0–0 draw at Wembley. The following season he made his debut for the England Under-21 side, becoming the first player to be selected without a league appearance to his name. Obviously too good a goalkeeper to understudy Peter Shilton at Forest, he joined Queens Park Rangers in

Chris Woods

the summer of 1979 and made his league debut in the opening game of the new season, a 2–0 home win over Bristol Rovers. An automatic first choice for one and a half seasons, he surprisingly lost his place to John Burridge and joined Norwich City. He was an ever-present at Carrow Road in four of his five seasons there and in 1984–85 won his second League Cup winners' medal. At the end of that season he won the first of 43 caps for England. Norwich, however, had been relegated and though they were promoted at the first attempt, Woods left to join Rangers for £600,000. In five years at Ibrox Park, he won four Scottish league championship medals and four Skol League Cup medals. Following the Scottish club's need to reduce its number of foreign players, he signed for Sheffield Wednesday for £1.2 million. In his early days at Hillsborough, he bore the brunt of the fans' wrath for some heavy defeats but in 1992–93 he kept 13 clean sheets, including three in a row. In recent seasons he has suffered a number of injuries and apart from a loan spell at Reading in 1995–96 has understudied Kevin Pressman for most of that time. However, when he has played he has shown flashes of the brilliance that made him one of the country's top-class goalkeepers.

WORLD CUP. In 1966, four World Cup matches were staged at Hillsborough. They were:

West Germany	5	Switzerland	0
Switzerland	1	Spain	2
Argentina	2	Switzerland	0
Uruguay	0	West Germany	4 (QF)

WORST START. The club's worst-ever start to a season was in 1977–78. It took 11 league games to record the first victory of the season, drawing five and losing five of the opening fixtures. The run ended with a 1–0 success over Chesterfield at Hillsborough with Tommy Tynan scoring the goal.

WORTHINGTON, NIGEL. Signed from Ballymena by Notts County manager Jimmy Sirrel in the summer of 1981, Nigel Worthington soon established himself at Meadow Lane and missed few matches before joining Sheffield Wednesday in February 1984. After helping the club to promotion, he won the first of his many caps for Northern Ireland against Wales in the penultimate match of the Home Championship. Apart from 1985–86 when he lost his place following injury to Glyn Snodin and then Chris Morris, Worthington was a regular first choice for Wednesday. He helped the Owls to win promotion in 1990–91 and was a member of the side that beat Manchester United 1–0 in that season's League Cup final. The Owls' most capped player, he had played in 417 first-team games for the club when in the summer of 1994 he joined Leeds United for £325,000. The vastly experienced Northern Ireland left-back spent two seasons at Elland Road filling in on the left side of the field when Dorigo or Speed were injured. He had appeared in 53 league and Cup games when, out of contract, he left United during the summer of 1996 and is now player–manager of Blackpool.

WRIGHT, JOCKY. Signed by Bolton Wanderers in the summer of 1895, after he had played in 18 games for Clyde in the Scottish Division, Jocky Wright was an ever-present in Bolton's first season at Burnden Park. He continued to be a regular in the side until Sheffield Wednesday paid £200 for him in October 1898. His debut for the Owls was in the famous game against Aston Villa which was abandoned 11 minutes from full-time because of bad light. The remaining time was played the following March. In 1899–1900, Wright was Wednesday's leading scorer with 26 goals as they gained promotion to the first division as champions of division two. After 110 games for Wednesday, he returned to Bolton but failed to find success as the club's 1902–03 campaign ended in relegation.

WYLDE, RODGER. Rodger Wylde made his league debut for Wednesday against Middlesbrough in November 1972, but had to wait until the appointment of Len Ashurst as manager before establishing himself in the side. In 1976–77, he ended the season as the club's top scorer with 25 league and Cup goals. Halfway through the Owls' promotion-winning season of 1979–80 he was allowed to leave and joined Oldham Athletic for £80,000. He scored 51 goals in 113 league games for the Boundary Park club before continuing his career with Sporting Lisbon, Sunderland, Barnsley, Rotherham United and Stockport County.

X

X. In football X traditionally stands for a draw. The club record for the number of draws in a season was in 1978–79 when they managed 19 draws out of 46 matches.

XMAS DAY. There was a time when league matches were regularly played on Christmas Day, but in recent years, the game's authorities have dropped the fixture from their calendar. The last time Sheffield Wednesday played on Christmas Day was in 1957 when they drew 4–4 at home to Preston North End. The first occasion that Wednesday played a league game on Christmas Day was 1893 when Bolton's goalkeeper Somerville punched the ball into his own nets to give the Owls a 1–1 draw. When Wednesday met Sheffield United in 1908, a George Simpson goal gave the Owls the points in a 1–0 win. It hasn't always been plain sailing for Wednesday on Christmas Day; in 1923, they lost 5–1 at Coventry City and the year after 6–2 at home to Blackpool. In 1929, Mark Hooper hit a Christmas Day hat–trick as Wednesday beat Everton 4–1 at Goodison Park.

Y

YOUNG, GERRY. Unfortunately, Gerry Young's name will always be associated with Wednesday's 1966 FA Cup final appearance against Everton, when he failed to cut out a long clearance, allowing Derek Temple to run on and score the winning goal. However, the popular Jarrow-born defender was a model professional and gave the club great service. He arrived at Hillsborough in May 1955 and made his first-team debut at Blackpool in March 1957. Over the next five seasons, he appeared in only 32 games, not winning a regular first-team place until Tony Kay joined Everton in 1962. In 1963–64, Gerry Young was the club's only ever-present as they finished sixth in the first division and in November 1964 he won his only England cap in a 2–1 win over Wales at Wembley. Due to make his second appearance against Holland a few weeks later, he ruptured his thigh in the match at White Hart Lane and was forced to miss 17 games. He gave up playing in 1971 after making 345 league and Cup appearances and joined the club's coaching staff. However, after taking temporary charge of team affairs, he was sacked when Steve Burtenshaw departed.

YOUNGEST PLAYER. The youngest player to appear in a first-class fixture for Sheffield Wednesday is goalkeeper Peter Fox, who played in the second division match against Orient (home

Peter Fox

2–0) on 31 March 1973 when he was 15 years 269 days old.

YOUTH CUP. Sheffield Wednesday have reached the FA Youth Cup final on just one occasion. In season 1990–91, the Owls' youth side beat Bury 4–1, Aston Villa 3–2, West Bromwich Albion 2–1, Hull City 5–1 (after two 1–1 draws) and Manchester United 2–1 on aggregate in the semi-final, before playing Millwall in the final. A crowd of 1,666 saw the young Owls side lose 3–0 at Hillsborough and though they drew the second-leg 0–0 at The Den, they had to be content with runners-up medals.

YO-YO YEARS. The 1950s have passed into the club's history as the 'yo-yo years' as Wednesday won promotion on no fewer than four occasions and suffered relegation three times. The Owls were promoted in 1949–50 but their stay in the first division lasted one season, for at the end of 1950–51, they were relegated. In 1951–52 they won the second division championship with Derek Dooley scoring 46 league goals in 30 games. After two seasons near the foot of the first division, Wednesday were eventually relegated in 1954–55, finishing nine points adrift of their relegation companions Leicester City. However, the Owls bounced back immediately, winning the second division championship in 1955–56. After finishing in mid-table in the top flight the following season, Wednesday suffered relegation again in 1957–58 without winning a single away game. In 1958–59, Wednesday won the second division championship to return to the first division for the fourth time in the 1950s.

Z

ZENITH. In the opening years of the century, Sheffield Wednesday won the first division title in consecutive seasons, the second victory being more emphatic than the first, but their hopes of a double floundered in the semi-final of the FA Cup in the season the league championship was retained. As it was between 1902 and 1904, so it was between 1928 and 1930. In 1928–29, Wednesday took the league championship with only 52 points, the lowest winning total from a 42 match programme. When Wednesday began their defence of the League title in August 1929, the line-up had a very familiar look about it. England international Jack Brown was in goal, missing only one game in the two championship-winning seasons. Loyal servants, England international Ernest Blenkinsop and Tommy Walker were the full-backs, whilst the engine-room of the side was the all-international half-back line of Alf Strange, Tony Leach and Billy Marsden. On the wings were Mark Hooper and Ellis Rimmer, whilst skipper Jimmy Seed and Jack Allen were joined in the forward line by the close-season signing, Harry Burgess from Stockport. The Owls were fortunate to have eight of that side play in at least 39 of the 42 games. No player missed more than ten games and no reserve needed to play more than nine times. After Portsmouth were beaten 4–0 on the opening day of the season, one of the highlights was a 7–2 thrashing handed out to

Manchester United, with Jack Allen scoring four of the goals. At the turn of the year, Wednesday were top of the table and as the season progressed, they effectively clinched the title over the Easter meetings against Derby County. After losing 4–1 at the Baseball Ground, a Jack Allen hat-trick helped the Owls avenge that defeat with a 6–3 victory. They won the title in style, finishing ten points clear of Derby County who were runners-up. Their goals tally of 105 was a new first division record, 21 ahead of the previous best and their 60 points equalled the previous record. In the FA Cup, Burnley were disposed of in round three by a Jack Allen goal, and the Wednesday inside-forward grabbed another two in a 4–2 win over second division Oldham Athletic. In the fifth round, a crowd of over 53,000 saw the Owls crush Bradford 5–1 before they were held to a 2–2 draw at Nottingham Forest in the quarter-finals. In the replay at Hillsborough, Wednesday triumphed 3–1 to reach the semi-finals for the first time since they won the trophy in 1907. The game against Huddersfield Town was played at Old Trafford and attracted a crowd of 69,292. The Owls took the lead through Mark Hooper after 21 minutes but Town equalised on the stroke of half-time. Yet despite having most of the play after the interval, it was Huddersfield who snatched the lead. With full-time approaching, Hooper crossed from the right to Allen, who crashed the ball into the net, but between Allen shooting and the ball crossing the line, the referee blew the final whistle.

ZENITH DATA SYSTEMS CUP. The Zenith Data Systems Cup replaced the Simod Cup in the 1989–90 season. Wednesday's first match in the competition saw them beat rivals and neighbours Sheffield United 3–2 after extra-time, but the Owls lost 4–1 at Middlesbrough in the third round. The team from Teeside went on to reach the final, where they lost 1–0 to Chelsea. In 1990–91, Wednesday were held to a 3–3 draw at Hillsborough by Barnsley, before the team from Oakwell won 4–2 on penalties. Wednesday last entered the competition in 1991–92 but after beating Manchester City 3–2, went out in the next round, losing 1–0 at Notts County.